James Relly

The Sadducee detected and refuted, in remarks on the works of

Richard Coppin

James Relly

The Sadducee detected and refuted, in remarks on the works of Richard Coppin

ISBN/EAN: 9783741197581

Manufactured in Europe, USA, Canada, Australia, Japa

Cover: Foto ©Andreas Hilbeck / pixelio.de

Manufactured and distributed by brebook publishing software
(www.brebook.com)

James Relly

The Sadducee detected and refuted, in remarks on the works of

Richard Coppin

THE

SADDUCEE

Detected and Refuted,

In REMARKS on the

WORKS

OF

RICHARD COPPIN.

BY
JAMES RELLY.

For the Sadducees *say, That there is no Resurrection, neither Angel, nor Spirit.* ACTS xxiii. 8.

LONDON:

Printed by M. LEWIS, at the *Bible and Dove*, in *Paternoster-Row.* 1764.

[Price One-Shilling.]

THough I greatly dislike the sentiments of *Richard Coppin,* yet their obsoleteness would have effectually secured them from my attacks: had they not been now re-published and sold, as it were under my nose; many of my hearers, being subscribers to the re-printing of them. From which circumstance, it being quite natural for the public to suppose that our doctrines are congenial; I thought it right to undeceive them: by giving them, in all these particulars, a specimen of my sentiments; which must necessarily be the sentiments of all such, who understand, and believe the doctrines which I preach. Unto this, with the desire of some friends, the following Remarks owe their existence: much rather then to any sanguine expectations by me entertained; of convincing such (of their error) who have already turned aside. For, where there is no heart for the authority of scripture, nor an ear to receive the arguments of reason, it is in vain for man to attempt the conviction and instruction of his brother: as objects of pity, all such must be left to the wis-

dom,

dom, power, and goodneſs of him that made them : and who only can convince them of their error.

As I am rather confident of my matter, than of my manner, I hope the candid reader will paſs over all faults of the latter, and attend particularly to the former, honouring it with their credit, as far as it confiſts with the ſcriptures and right reaſon.

THE

THE

SADDUCEE

Detected and Refuted, &c.

My Dear FRIENDS,

CONTROVERSY is not my element:
yet, if (in the fmalleft degree) it will
contribute to your pleafure, and fatif-
faction, for me to caft my mite into the
treafury, I fhall readily comply with your
defire.

You defire me to give you, and the public,
my opinion of *Coppin*'s works; as they are now
re-publifhing.

That I might be able to do this fincerely and
impartially, I applied myfelf with the utmoft
care, and candor, to the reading of them.—I
read three numbers of a work, intitled, *Michael's
oppofing the dragon*, &c. and alfo another
book by the fame author, intitled, *The advancement of all things in Chrift, and of Chrift in all
things*: prefaced with a warm recommendation
by Mr. *Cayley*.

A 3   Having

Having thus far qualified myfelf to give you an anfwer*, I fhall firft tell you, as a matter not at all foreign to your enquiry, that I was not in the leaft degree acceffary, no, nor fo much as privy, to the prefent re-publication of *Coppin's* works, or to any part thereof.

As to the author, I think him unneceffarily abftrufe : He labours to cloath himfelf with darknefs as with a garment, and carefully avoids fpeaking intelligibly, except when he rails at his antagonifts : and then he ufes great plainnefs of fpeech. But, to darken counfel, with words without knowledge, is the grand arcanum of myfticifm : and by fome, reckoned to be the infallible criterion of fpiritual teach-ings : witnefs Mr. *Cayley's* preface, to part of this author's works.

Again, inftead of fubmitting, when pinched by argument, or manifeftly oppofed by truth, he is very evafive : and often begs the queftion, that he may have an opportunity of befpatter-ing his adverfary, and of giving his own fyf-tem an air of plaufibility.

One inftance of this, I fhall give you, out of the many that may be gathered from his works, No. 3. chap. 12. of *Michael oppofing the dragon.* Where, (becaufe his opponents argue for the refurrection of the fame body) he infinuates that they plead for the refurrection of a finful body : whereas there was nothing farther from their thoughts : and this he very well knew.

If

---

* It was fuppofed by many, and even affirmed by fome, that I privately encouraged the re-publication of *Coppin's* works. Which accounts for my manner of fpeaking above.

If I affirm, that the fame body that died, and
was buried, fhall rife again : doth it follow
from thence, that it muft rife a finful body?
I muft deny it, except *Coppin* had proved, or,
that his admirers will yet prove, that fin is a
property, or part of the body, and effential to
its exiftence—And that would be juft the fame
as to fay, that a leprofy, a fever, a delirium,
being diforders in the body, are a part thereof;
and that the body cannot exift without them.

Again, I think him opinionated, and con-
ceited, even to fillynefs : as appears from his
boaftings of light, knowledge, purity, &c.
above his fellows ; though there is not the leaft
fpark of this pre-eminence difcoverable : neither
in his fpirit, nor manner.

As to that infallibility which he pretends to,
in all his filly, unfcriptural determinations ; I
believe every man of fenfe, will attribute it to
pride and ignorance. Though he affects to treat
his opponents in a very fupercilious manner,
yet he cannot help difcovering, that their accu-
fations give him fmart. He betrays a much
greater fondnefs for himfelf, than becomes an
apoftle : by complaining of his perfecutions,
&c. But I fhall now leave the author, and
take notice of his doctrines.

In his book, intitled, *The advancement of all
things in Chrift* ; (the fame which Mr. *Cayley*
hath authorized, and bleffed with the higheft
encomiums) he begins with this hypothefis :
That there are two principles, or qualities, in
man; which he calls good, and evil: and that
thefe principles are the elect, and reprobate;
the believer, and unbeliever; the faved, and

the

the damned; the *Jacob* and *Efau*; the *Chrift*,
&c. in every man. And, that the Perfons of
mankind are not at all concerned in any of
thofe characters. For faith he, " God hates
" no man's perfon, but the evil in the perfon :
" neither doth he love any man's perfon any
" farther than as they fhew forth fomething of
" himfelf."

This is not only unfupported by fcripture,
and common fenfe; but diametrically oppofite
to both. Doth the word of truth ever affirm,
or even fuppofe, that there is any good in man?
did the prophets, our Saviour, or his apoftles,
ever bear fuch a teftimony? Is it not their con-
ftant language, that the imaginations of man's
heart are evil, and that continually? that there
is none, who doth good, no not one? that we
are all as an unclean thing, and all our righteoufnefs are as filthy rags? that there is none
good but one, even God? and that all the
deeds of this world are evil? that in our flefh
(or perfon) there dwells no good thing?

And as to the fuppofition of the principles of
good, and evil, refiding in man; the fame word
of truth enquires, *What fellowfhip hath righteoufnefs with unrighteoufnefs, and what communion hath
light with darknefs, what concord hath Chrift with*
Belial, *or what part hath he that believeth with
an infidel?*

If thefe cannot dwell together in the fame
houfe, much lefs can they dwell together in the
fame heart; in the fame perfon. Our Saviour
tells us, that the fame perfon cannot ferve two
mafters, *i. e.* God and mammon. The apoftle
faith, that the fame fountain cannot fend forth
bitter

bitter waters and sweet. Thus the scriptures detest, and explode, the notion of those principles being in man.

For, if the same person be an habitation in common; for God and the Devil, for *Christ* and *Belial*, for light and darkness; then would the apostles be found false witnesses: the same fountain would then send forth bitter waters and sweet: *Christ* and *Belial* would then have concord: and the believer would have part with an infidel.

Again, it is contrary to experience, to suppose the being of those two principles in man. The prophets, and apostles, all confessed, that they were sinners; and that there dwelt no good thing in them. Their good consisted wholly in that which dwelt in *Christ* : in what he was made of God unto them—and which was revealed in them by the Spirit of truth.

Every christian, in every age, who have truly known themselves ; *have* confessed, and *do* confess, that according to the propensities of their own hearts, they are carnal and sold under sin : and that in them, in their flesh, or in their own persons ; there dwelleth no good thing.

That all men are sinners, their actions, spirit, and manner, fully prove: We judge of this, according to what we are taught, to conceive of the nature, and properties, of the divine Being: and, if we are to judge by this rule, it is obvious even to common sense, that there is none that doth good, no not one.

The supposed good, in man; is quite invisible: If you believe it, you must believe it unseen: you must take their word, for what
they,

they, to a judicious eye, to an unbiaſſed judgment, can never make appear. So that if God loves no man, but in proportion to the good that is in him, we may look upon the eternal ruin of every creature as inevitable.

This antichriſtian invention, owes its original to that ſpirit, which attempts to inveſtigate truth by the fluctuating paſſions: by frames, and viſions, rather than by the teſtimony of the prophets and apoſtles.

The ſelf-righteous ſpirit was alſo deeply concerned in the ſcheme: when fondly dreaming of goodneſs, and holineſs, in the creature; and at the ſame time convinced of the evil, by ſcripture and experience; there remained no other way of ſolving the difficulty, but by propoſing that there are two principles in man: or two diſtinct qualities, *i. e.* good, and evil.

Nor has oppoſition to the true *Chriſt* been wanting here. As appears from its aſcribing to this phantaſm in man; the whole of the ſalvation, and characters of the Lord *Jeſus:* which I ſhall have occaſion to ſhew, more particularly, in my following remarks.

Having denied, that the perſons of mankind are either the objects of God's love, or hatred; that they are either the ſubjects of ſalvation, or condemnation, he, to maintain ſome ſhadow of conſiſtency, denies alſo the reſurrection of the body: No. 3. page 67.—So does he the aſcenſion of our Saviour's body, if not his reſurrection, in No. 2. ch. 9. in which, he has falſified the ſcriptures, and made void the hopes of the children of God from the beginning.

To

To do this, with impunity ; he pretends
that the fcriptures are an allegory—that there
are allegories in the fcriptures, I deny not. But
they do not deftroy facts; and make void the
truth of relation, and narrative, contained
therein : *Paul*, fpeaking of *Abraham*'s affair with
the bond-woman, calls it indeed an allegory—
but *Paul*, in fo faying, does not deny that there
was fuch a perfon as *Abraham*, nor that he had
a fon by a flave : but his allegory confifted in a
fpiritual doctrine, concealed under that fact ;
until revealed to him by the Holy Ghoft.

Where allegories have no affinity to facts,
and to facts properly ftated, and afcertained ;
the man who attempts to build by them, is as
though he attempted to build cafties in the air :
Such kind of a building is *Coppin*'s : who will
have it, that the refurrection, and afcenfion of
the Lord *Chrift*, is to be underftood fpiritually
or allegorically only.

This brings to my remembrance, the dream
of a certain vifionary, who would be an in-
ftructor of others : This perfon, not long fince,
being in company where the fiege of *Samaria*
was talked of, of what diftreffes the inhabitants
felt, how a woman in the rage and fury of
hunger eat her own child, *&c.* The fame perfon,
then afked, with a contemptuous fmile, whether they thought the thing *literally* true, or not ?
Upon their anfwering in the affirmative, the
perfon replied : It is not true in your fenfe ;
I myfelf am the *Samaria :* and have
been fo very ftraitly befieged ; that I was
obliged to eat my firft-born, *i. e.* that inward

goodnefs

goodnefs, which I had brought forth in forrow; and until then had nourifhed fo carefully.

But to return; I confefs myfelf fimple e-nough to believe all things that are written in the law, and in the prophets; and that I have hope towards God, that there fhall be a refurrection of the dead: I particularly reverence the tefti-mony of the evangelifts, concerning *Jefus Chrift* our Lord. And in them we learn, that our Sa-viour was God incarnate, God manifeft in the flefh, the word made flefh, *&c.* and that he was a real man; he had a reafonable foul, and a material body: that from infancy to a perfect ftate of manhood, he lived upon this earth; going about doing good, and fulfilling all righteoufnefs. And, that as a man, he felt pain, ficknefs, wearinefs, hunger, thirft, joy, forrow, *&c.* That in the article of his fuffer-ings, his foul was forrowful, even to death; whilft his body was fcourged, crowned with thorns, fpit upon, buffeted, and treated with the utmoft indignity. And after all, by many wounds, he was nailed to a crofs; where, having vented ftrong cries and tears, he expired under the torment. That, when dead, he was taken down from the crofs and laid in a fepul-chre, wherein never man was laid before—that a guard of foldiers was appointed to watch the tomb, left his difciples fhould fteal him away—that on the third morning, notwithftanding all their pre-caution, the angels defcended; and fmiting the keepers with deadly fear, rolled the ftone from the mouth of the tomb: (this was altogether unneceffary if the material body did not rife again)—that the very identical body of

our

our Saviour, which was laid in that grave, did then arife ; and fhewed himfelf alive to his difciples. All this I affuredly believe. He firft convinced his difciples of the truth of his refurrection, by his well-known form and features; by his voice, manner and matter of fpeech. He fecondly fhewed them the wounds in his hands and his feet, by which he had been nailed to the crofs : as they well knew how he had been treated ; thofe marks, being perfectly correfpondent, fhewed them it was he. Thirdly, he propofed to *Thomas* (who was the moft incredulous of them all) in the prefence of the ten, that he fhould put his hand into his fide, and his fingers into the nail-prints : and to them all, he propofed that they fhould handle him, and fee, for that a fpirit had not flefh and bones, as they might perceive him to have.

He converfed with them, he eat and drank in their prefence ; and gave them every poffible and neceffary proof of his refurrection, in that material, individual, identical body ; which was crucified and laid in the fepulchre. After continuing with them for the fpace of forty days, he, (in their prefence, before their eyes) lifting up his hands and bleffing them, afcended up on high : an intervening cloud receiving him out of their fight. And they were then told, *that that fame* Jefus *fhould come in like manner as they had feen him afcend.*

Now, as it is manifeft, that he retained the identity, and corporeity of his body, to the moment of his afcenfion ; it belongs to the oppofers to tell us what became of his body, if it did not afcend ; what mountain, or hill, was it found upon afterwards? did it diſſolve into air? or is it preſerved ſomewhere until he come again? (becauſe they were taught, that he ſhould come again, in like manner as they had ſeen him aſcend) If it is, let them tell us where? Did not the manner wherein they ſaw him aſcend, and in which he was to come again, relate to the reality of his perſon, and the method of his aſcent? and alſo to their ſeeing him with their bodily eyes? I think it did: Let ſuch who think the contrary, convince me of my error, if they can.

Again, if the body of *Chriſt* did not aſcend, it will be pretty difficult to affix a meaning to the term: It cannot be applied to the godhead; the nature and properties of which, denies all circumſcription and paſſibility: nor can it be applied to the human ſoul only, for reaſons given below *.

To

---

* The terms *deſcend*, and *aſcend*, implies; either a change of ſtate, or change of place, or both. But the godhead as omnipreſent, impaſſible, unchangeable, &c. cannot admit of change in either: Therefore, theſe terms cannot plied to our Saviour reſpecting his godhead only—Nor have they a limited application to his ſoul: becauſe it doth not appear, that our Saviour ever manifeſted his perſon, glory, his ſalvation, but as in the matter and form of a human body.—He is repreſented as inhabitant in ſuch a body, at the formation of *Adam*—when, as the image and likeneſs of God; he was alſo the firſt born, and the beginning of his creation; exhibiting in himſelf, the model after which man was to be created. In the form, and manner, of a human body, he appeared unto *Abraham*—in the ſame manner, and form, he wreſtled with *Jacob*—in the ſame likeneſs he appeared to *Moſes*, *Joſhua*, *Job*, *Iſaiah*, &c. And in ſuch a body he always manifeſted himſelf unto his apoſtles, as well after his retur-

To turn all the fcripture-account of our Saviour's refurrection, and afcenfion, into fuch
an allegory, as deftroys the facts; is juft the
fame, as if they denied that there ever was
fuch a perfon as *Paul* the apoftle : but that all
that is faid of him, relates to certain difpenfa-
tions which mankind pafs under in their own
minds. And again, in hiftory; it is as though
we fhould aver, that there never was fuch a
perfon as our king *Harry* the fifth : but, that
the tradition of fuch a perfon, and of his bat-
tles, and victories in *France*; relate altogether
to the good principle in man, the divine power
fighting and conquering in the *France* of our
nature.

What would be our conceptions of fuch a
ranting fpirit as this, madly drawing every
thing into that devouring vortex, HIMSELF ? I
believe, that the moft charitable conftructions

we

---

refurrection, as before : and in the fame manner doth the
Holy Ghoft now reveal him : when he takes of the things
which are his, and fhews them unto us; Hence it is manifeft, that the Lord Jefus always occupied a human body;
both in matter, and form : particularly in his defcenfion and
afcenfion. When he defcended to a fellow-feeling with the
creatures, even to the loweft depth of human mifery; it was
in the whole man, confifting of body and foul. When he
defcended into torment, where the pangs of death encompaffed
him round about, and the pains of hell gat hold upon him;
it was as the whole man, confifting of body and foul. In
the fame fenfe he defcended into the chambers of death, ex-
ploring the fides of the pit; and finking to the lower parts
of the earth. The apoftle affures us that, he that defcended;
is the fame alfo that afcended, up far above all heavens.
Upon which authority, we affirm; that the body of the Lord
Jefus is rifen from the dead, and afcended up on high—
otherwife he who defcended, is not the fame that afcended.

we could poffibly put upon fuch fentiments, would amount to this : The poor creature is altogether under the baneful influence of ignorance and pride.

And is not this the cafe with the author, whofe writings are the fubject of my prefent confideration, and indeed with the myftics in general ? do not they pretend to account for the truth of all things in themfelves ? They certainly draw all fcripture-facts, fuch as the incarnation, perfonality, birth, life, fufferings, death, refurrection, and afcenfion of *Chrift* ; into their own vortex : and deny their reality, or at leaft their ufefulnefs in any other fenfe.

I need not ufe many arguments to prove, that whilft a man, by fuch a conduct, betrays the moft wretched ignorance of himfelf : he alfo gives evidence fufficient, of his being one of the children of pride. The bleffed *Jefus* faith of himfelf, I am the truth. But the perfon abovementioned, contefts the point with him : by declaring that the truth of all things is to be looked for in man. And thus as a thief and a robber, he fteals the brighteft jewel in *Immanuel*'s crown ; to ornament felf with.

Allow but the facts of the refurrection, and afcenfion of our Saviour's body ; and then you may fpiritualize as much, as high, as refined as you pleafe upon it ; provided you always crown the head, by keeping the pre-eminence and exaltation of our Saviour's perfon in view : otherwife, the fpirit which is in you, with all its niceties and appearances of piety, is but an antichrift.

If

If the refurrection of our Saviour's body, be
afcertained in the fcriptures; and guaranteed
by all the apoftles, as it furely is; we may eafily come to a determination, concerning the refurrection and future ftate of our own bodies:
for the apoftle tells us, that our bodies fhall be
fafhioned like unto the glorious body of the Son
of God. The New-Teftament teaches us, that
the refurrection of the Lord *Jefus*, his ftate,
as then appearing and manifefting himfelf, is the
perfect pattern, and fample of our ftate and con-
dition eternally with God.

What does the term refurrection imply, if
not the rifing again to life, of that which was
fubjected to death? But the foul is immortal,
as proved from fcripture and reafon, and cannot die. It is the body *only* that dies: Therefore the future refurrection of the dead, if there
be any, muft be that of the body, and of the
body only: otherwife there is no meaning in
the term.

I confefs that the term is fometimes ufed in
the fcriptures, as refpecting the raifing again of
mankind in the fecond *Adam*; from that death
of trefpaffes and fin, wherein they were involved
in the firft *Adam*. There are thofe alfo, who
apply it to that quickening, or renewal, which
is effected and wrought in the fpirit of the mind,
through the manifeftation of the truth.

To limit and confine the term to this, is certainly to deny a future refurrection, and to
commence difciples of *Hymeneus* and *Philetus*;
of whom hear what the apoftle *Paul* faith:
Their word will eat as doth a canker, who con-
B   *cerning*

cerning the truth, have erred; saying, that the resurrection is passed already: and overthrow the faith of some. For an Infidel, a Deist, to set up his own opinions in opposition to the apostle, is not to be wondered at : but for people professing themselves Christians, who acknowledge the spirit speaking by the apostles, to be infallible : for such to prefer the instigations of a private spirit, to the public testimony of the divine word : is very strange and inconsistent.

For my own part, I do not see that death dissolves the union between soul and body, any more than what sleep doth. In sleep, the body is passive and inactive, as in a state of death : and yet the union of soul and body is discoverable in sleep.—So also in epileptic fits, *&c.* when the body is deprived of motion, and senseless as a corpse; when all the channels of advice are stopt, and the common sensorium deprived of intelligence : the soul doth *then* evidence her own existence; and confesses her union to the body, by retaining its organs : which she occupies in the spiritual world; (of which world the soul herself is a native) though according to things present, she hath ceased from the exercise of the material eye, ear, hands, *&c.*

Death being only a sleep, a state of suspension, respecting the exercise of bodily functions, destroys not the unity of soul and body; nor does it hinder, but that the soul possesses the bodily organs, in her consciousness of unity to the body.

Should

Should it be objected, that death is such a
sleep as destroys the body: I answer, The
change, or alteration of the body in death, re-
pects form and manner only, and doth not imply the loss of matter: or that it loseth its identity: And therefore, I deny that death anni-
hilates the body. The scriptures speak of man,
as consisting of three parts: body, soul, and
spirit. The body is meerly material, earthly,
inactive and senseless: And yet the body itself,
is fearfully and wonderfully made: That wisdom, power, and glory which manifest themselves, in the exquisite workmanship and struc-
ture of the human body, effectually demon-
strate that it was built for eternity; and not for
a moment of time only.

The second part of man, called his spirit, is
his senses: This spirit, dwells *in*, and is united
unto the whole body; even *in*, and unto every
minute part thereof. This spirit, is guardian to
the body, discovers bodily dangers, and con-
cerns itself for the prevention of them. It also
discovers what is good for the body, assenting
to it, and chusing it. This is the spirit, that
immediately occupies the bodily organs in this
material world. It hears through the ear; it
sees through the eye; it smells through the
nostrils; it tastes through the palate; it feels
through the skin: and swifter than lightning,
it sends intelligence of all its discoveries to the
common sensorium: where, in the head, as in
the pre-eminent member, the spirit hath its
highest residence: according to the determinations there, which are as speedily communica-

ted

ted to the whole; the paffions predominate: either love, joy, forrow, hatred, anger, &c. Thus far this fpirit is in common to men and brutes.

But this fpirit in man, as dwelling in, and united unto every minute part of his body, is alfo united to his foul: And thus becomes the medium of unity between foul and body, in the rational creature.

The foul in man, is an immortal confciouf-nefs of exiftence, having the powers of think-ing, reafoning, reflection, will, refolution, &c. — This foul, united to the animal fpirit in man; improves, and raifes that fpirit in him, much above what it is in the brutes. Thus, though the faculty of fpeech be in common to man and other creatures, as birds, &c: yet the latter has not the power of invention, order and reafon, and can only fpeak at random what they hear. But man has reafon, invention, order and defign in his fpeech: which proves, that the principal, or head of the triad, in his compofition; is a fpiritual dignity.

As the foul in man, is immediately united to the fpirit, and the fpirit to the body; I would obferve, that the foul always retains the fpi-rit: Hence it is faid, that the fpirit of a man goeth upward (i. e. in conjunction with the foul which is divine) whilft the fpirit of a beaft (as not having a divine and immortal foul) go-eth downward.

As the foul, in man, retains the fpirit, and lifts it upward with herfelf—fo does the Spirit al-fo retain the body, in its organical fyftem: even when

when the material machinery is fubjected to corruption, and ferment in the grave *.

In a dream, when the body is as dead, the
foul, by the medium of the animal fpirit, occupies its organs; and feels the paffions, fometimes to very great degree. Nor, doth the body's being in the grave, hinder the foul, (who
by the medium of the fpirit, holds the body in
union through all its changes) from fo retaining the organical fyftem thereof, as to feel the
paffions ; as perfectly at leaft as fhe does in a
dream—for which reafon, the apoftle with the
utmoft propriety calls death a fleep.

And here, it may not be improper to obferve,
that fleep doth not always imply reft. There
is a fleep; which, with very unpleafant dreams,
extreamly troubles the mind; and fatigues the
body: Tired, diftreffed, and tormented ; we
find gladnefs in awakening from fuch a fleep;
and reft, in reflecting that our mifery was but a
dream.

I have been credibly informed, by fome who
have undergone the operation ; that after the
amputation of a difeafed member, the patient
has felt pain, (in every particular to their fenfes) as if in the feparated limb : juft as though

B 3   it

---

* May we not fuppofe that the foul, by the medium of
the animal fpirit, may (even after death) retain the body:
refpecting its mode, and its neceffary conjunction ; for the
operations of the foul: in a manner ineffable, and peculiar
to fuch a ftate ? whence through the organs thereof, as fuited
to the fpiritual world; the foul may be capable of hearing,
feeing, feeling, &c. and alfo of *appearance* in an ærial, or
fhadowy form: and of fubjection to the paffions—fo far, as
to render her fufceptible of joy, or mifery, in a future ftate ?

it was yet in union with the body. The truth of this I fhall not attempt to inveftigate here : Yet I profefs to fee no caufe, why the foul, through the animal fpirit, may not, according to the laws and powers of union ; feel as *by* and *in* the body, though the latter according to fenfe be put off : And if fo, the foul cannot but long for the time; when the body having undergone its neceffary ferment, fhall be raifed in glory and immortality ; like unto that of the fon of God : a fit habitation for a fpirit to dwell in.

We look for the reality of all the joys, and reprefentations, which we have. in dreams ; un · to thofe that we have when · awake : when the whole machinery is in exercife. So may departed fpirits look forwards, from their vifionary enjoyments : for perfeftion, for confummate blifs, to the reftitution of all things. When the body fhall be raifed ; when the creature itfelf fhall be reftored from the bondage of corruption, and brought into the glorious liberty of the fons of God—when the redemption (to wit, that of the body) fhall be fully come— when every feed fhall have its own body.

The apoftle faith, *If ye be Chrift's, then are ye Abram's feed*—And elfewhere, fpeaking of our Saviour, he faith, that *he took upon him the feed of* Abram—And again, that we are *one flefh* with 'him—that we are *his fulnefs*—that we are *members of his body, of his flefh, and of his bones.* From thefe, and many other teftimonies in the divine word, it appears that we are comprehended in *Chrift :* our bodies, in his body ; and our

our fouls, in his foul: He being in himfelf, the fountain of lives.

If it be true then, that *Chrift* faved himfelf, in the whole man, confifting of body and foul; as his refurrection fufficiently demonftrates: then were *our* bodies, faved in *his* body; and *our* fouls, in *his* foul. Unto which falvation, *i. e.* of *our* fouls, in *his* foul; we come up even in *this* life—when through the knowledge of the truth, we attain to the *end of our faith*. But we are yet obliged to wait, for the redemption: to wit, that of the body. We cannot come up, in the prefent ftate of things, according to our bodies, to the ftate of *Chrift's* perfect body: Therefore the apoftle fays, *We look for the Saviour, the Lord Jefus Chrift; who fhall change our vile body.*

But, if the redemption of our fouls, in the foul of *Chrift*, did not deftroy their individuality; nor prevent their being brought up, through the knowledge of the truth, unto the enjoyment of that falvation, which they had in his foul: Wherefore, fhould it be fuppofed, that notwithstanding the redemption of our bodies, in his body, *they* muft lofe their individuality, *they* muft not rife again, nor be brought up to inherit that falvation which they have in the body of *Chrift?* Let me fay, as there was a time for the one; fo there remains a time for the other: when the whole man fhall be faved; when both in body and foul, he fhall be for ever with the Lord.

Again, the practice of thofe who deny the refurrection of the body, gives their opinion the lie. Why are they fo remarkably fond of their bodies? to feed them, to drefs them, to

beautify

beautify them, to preferve them in health and
vigour, to honour them—and to gratify their
appetites, is the whole employment of life—
what are all the cares, and toils of life, directed to, but to the body? Man, can reap no
other advantage, than food, and cloathing,
from all his labours beneath the fun.

What fools then, to make fuch a momentary
being, as the body; the fole object of our care
and concern! And to be fo very unwilling to
part with them; which excepting lunacy, is
manifeftly the cafe with every man: *No man
hateth his own body.* I will fuppofe that the
apoftle, who bare this teftimony, had at leaft,
as much underftanding as a man, and as much
divine light and real piety, as a Chriftian;
as *Coppin*; his admirers; or, as any myftic
whatever—And yet he, though he knew; that
he had a building of God; an houfe not made
with hands, eternal in the heavens: and was defirous of being cloathed upon, with that garment
of immortality: (I fay) though he was well
affured of this, yet he fays, *not for that we would
be uncloathed—but cloathed upon, that mortality
might be fwallowed up of life.* By which, he
means as I fuppofe, that he was not defirous of
being found naked: by the lofs of his body—
but his defire was to be cloathed upon—both
body, and foul, with that glory and immortali-
ry which God had prepared for him.

And again, he faith in another place, *Behold
I fhew you a myftery; we fhall not all fleep, but
we fhall all be changed, in a moment, in the twinkling of an eye, at the laft trump. (For the trumpet
fhall found, and the dead fhall be raifed incorruptible;*

ble; and we shall be changed.) I apprehend his
meaning in those words, to be, that such who
are alive, at the end of time, shall not die: but
that they shall cease from all vile, earthly qualities, in a moment; in the twinkling of an eye:
The body shall be purified, and changed, without putting it off: into an incorruptible state—
*The dead shall be raised incorruptible, and we shall
be changed.* He not only assures us here, of the
body's being saved, and of its entering into
glory: but also of its salvation, and entrance
into bliss, without tasting death.

Should some poor anchorite in the desart,
consumed with famine, exposed to cold, and
nakedness, sinking under his infirmities, and
whose whole life in the body, is one continual
penance. I say, should such an one deny the
resurrection of the body, as not feeling much
consolation from its existence: it would have
some appearance. But for those, whose time,
labour, and study, are spent altogether on account of the body; and whose chief felicity in
life, seems to consist in gratifying its appetites.
I say, for such to deny its future bliss, and to
treat it only as a pampered beast, whereon they
ride for a season, is to act a very unreasonable,
and inconsistent part.

But so it is: The child of affliction believing,
that his poor famished or diseased body shall rise
again, and be fashioned like unto the glorious
body of the son of God; he lays it down in
hope—whilst the worldly, jolly, pretended-spi-
ritual man—the refined genius, as he would be
thought—(though possibly he hath not one ab-
stracted idea, of existence, separate from the
body)

body) unreasonably suggests, that the body being meerly brutal; shall as such, perish in death everlastingly.

Because the scriptures say, *That flesh and blood shall not inherit the kingdom of God.*— And that *being sown a natural body, it is raised a spiritual body:* there are those who infer, that the body shall not rise again. But I would observe, that the terms flesh, and blood, as used in the scriptures; doth not always imply, the material body. Sometimes it intends man's natural wisdom, understanding, and reason; as where our Saviour says to *Peter, Flesh and blood hath not revealed those things unto thee—but my Father which is in heaven.* Are there any so stupid, as to imagine that the Lord meant, thy body has not revealed those things unto thee? Upon a serious consideration I hope there are none such.

Again, the term intends ease, honour, and profit, according to this world. Hence the apostle tells us, that when it pleased God to reveal his son in him, he conferred not with flesh and blood: but gave himself up to preach *Jesus* unto the *Heathen.*

Again, it intends our own righteousnesses.— The apostle *Paul,* calls his circumcision on the eighth day—his being of the stock of *Israel*—his being of an orthodox, and respectable sect—his zeal in his religion—his blameless righteousness as touching the law. I say, he calls all this *flesh.* And in this sense the divine evangelist understood it: When speaking of the sons of God, he tells us, that *they were born, not of blood, nor of the will of the flesh, &c. Paul* uses the term flesh, in the same sense, in another place, where

he

he fays, *So then, they that are in the flefh, can-not pleafe God.* And again, *having begun in the Spirit, are ye now made perfect by the flefh.* But *Paul* does not mean, that they that are in the body, cannot pleafe God—becaufe he tells us elfewhere, that *Enoch, before his tranflation, had this teftimony, that he pleafed God.*

At other times the term is not limited to our fuppofed excellencies, *&c.* but ufed in a more indefinite fenfe; including all the weakneffes, frailties, and corruption of our mortal ftate—and in this fenfe it is ufed in the abovemention-ed text, *i. e.* flefh and blood cannot inherit the kingdom of God. It is evident, that the apo-ftle does not apply the term in thofe words, to the material body ; nor did he intend to deny the refurrection thereof. But his defign was to fhew the neceffity of the body's being purged, through death, from all the bafe qualities and infirmities, which conftitute what he terms flefh and blood ; and which, he fays, cannot inherit the kingdom of God.

He explains himfelf more fully in the follow-ing words—*Neither doth corruption inherit incor-ruption.* But we are not pleading for the refur-rection of a corrupt body—nay, we fhould then gain nothing by the change. The body of man, as the immediate creation of God, was incor-rupt—corruption as applied to man, in body or mind, certainly intends, the evil bias, and vile propenfities of human nature. Or, if by a cor-rupt body, we underftand, its purulency, its liablenefs to putrefaction—I would obferve that the latter, is only an effect of the former. And that it neither is effential to the being, or ex-

iftence,

iftence, of the body nor foul : Corruption in the
firft fenfe, is an accident only in man, and no
part of him ; and difeafe, death, or corruption,
in the fecond fenfe, is to be confidered, meerly,
as the effect or confequence of the former, and
can only fubfift by it ; and *where* that is found.
Chrift being made fin for us, fuftained corruption in the firft fenfe ; but as he totally eradica-
ted it, put it away, and deftroyed it ; by his
fufferings, and death, he did not fee corruption
in the fecond fenfe : that is, his body did not
putrify, nor moulder to duft—Thou wilt not
fuffer thy holy one to fee corruption.

But our bodies are not thus privileged, becaufe they are vile, flefh and blood, or corruption dwells in them—They like the houfe that
had the leprofy in the walls, muft be taken
down for the deftruction of the plague. We
who make our exit, before the time of the end,
muft fee corruption, becaufe our bodies are vile.
But we are taught that they fhall be raifed in
incorruption : yea, we have the pattern exhibited in perfection, in the glorious body of our divine *Immanuel :* In him, we view the glorious
reality, of what we are *with* God, and *to* God,
and of what we fhall be, *in*, and *unto* ourfelves,
when raifed from the dead.

As to the propofition, that the body is fown
natural, and raifed fpiritual. I would obferve,
that natural and fpiritual, are diftinct and oppofite *qualities* only ; and not diftinct beings.
Therefore, the change from natural to fpiritual,
doth not imply, that one being is loft, nor that
one being becomes another : but it implies, that
all thofe qualities which conftituted the natural
character,

character, being deftroyed in death, the body
rifes in the qualities which conftitute the fpiritual character. And thus the body is fown a
natural body; and raifed a fpiritual body:
Firft, the body is natural from its manner of
fubfifting, as by meats, drinks, fleep, &c.
Again, it is natural from its infirmities; fuch as
hunger, thirft, wearinefs, pain, ficknefs, and
death. Again, the body is natural from its affections, and operations, as generation, augmen-
tation, motion, &c.

The body as fubject to thefe, is a natural
body; but having put off (by death) all thefe,
it becomes a fpiritual body; a body fubfifting
without the ufe of natural means; fuch as
meats, drinks, fleep, phyfic, &c. A body free
from all infirmities, and from all earthly affections, and operations. A body, though retaining its materiality, yet in the refurrection as
the angels of God.

Know you not, faith the apoftle, that your
bodies are members of *Chrift* ? Shall I then take
the members of *Chrift,* and make them the
members of an harlot? God forbid. To which
I may fay, fhall we take the members of *Chrift*
and deftroy them? fhall we affert, that they
have no pre-eminence above a beaft, but that
they muft perifh everlaftingly? God forbid.

When *Lazarus* died, and *Jefus* approached to
raife him from the dead, one of the fifters of
the deceafed, went forth to meet him; and in
reverence to the Saviour (whilft fhe bewailed
her departed brother) fhe faid, *Lord, if thou
hadft been here, my brother had not died.* Unto
which, the compaffionate High-Prieft anfwered,

ed, *Thy brother shall rise again. Yea Lord,* (said
she) *I know that he shall rise again in the resurrection at the last day.* Jesus replied, *I am
the resurrection and the life; he that believeth
on me, though he were dead, yet shall he live:
And whosoever liveth, and believeth on me, shall
never die. Believest thus this? She said unto him,
Yea Lord.* That *Martha* believed the resurrection of the body at the last day, is declared in
words as expressive as can possibly be used:
nor did our Saviour reprove her sentiment (for
it is highly probable that she had received it
from him) he only taught her, that the resurrection of the human body, doth not proceed
from natural consequences, but that it depend-
ed altogether upon him. *I am the resurrection
and the life,* saith he. The fact of our Saviour's resurrection, doth not only ascertain that
of ours; exhibiting the most glorious and
shining pattern thereof; but it is also the cause,
the means and security of our resurrection. It
may also denote that power, wherewith he, as
the Son of man, stands invested by the Father.
Martha believed that her brother should rise a-
gain at the last day: But our Saviour
taught her, that as her brother could not rise
then, without him who was the resurrection and
the life: so neither was his power confined to
that day; but that he could exert it when it
pleased him so to do : and which he then intended to do, by raising her brother from the
grave.

It is said of the apostles, that they *preached,
through Jesus, the resurrection from the dead.*
And again of *Paul,* that *he preached Jesus,*
and

and the refurrection: and when they heard of the refurrection, fome mocked. Of the hope and re-furrection of the dead, (faith the fame apoftle) *am I called in queftion.* Again, *That there fhall be a refurrection of the dead, both of the juft, and of the unjuft.* Our Saviour faith, *The hour is coming, in which all that are in their graves fhall hear his voice, and fhall come forth: they that have done good, unto the refurrection of life; and they that have done evil, unto the refurrection of damnation. And the graves were opened, and many bodies of faints which flept, arofe and came out of the graves, and went into the holy city and appeared unto many.*—*If the dead rife not, then is not Chrift raifed; our faith is vain, and our preaching vain; ye are yet in your fins.* A-bram *accounted, that God was able to raife up* Ifaac, even *from the dead.* But not to multi-ply citations, it is manifeft, that the refurrec-tion of the body, is poffitively and clearly taught in the New-Teftament: and was a prin-cipal article in the preaching of the apoftles.

But fome man, fuch as *Coppin*, and his ad-mirers, will fay, How are the dead raifed up? and with what body do they come? Thou fool, faith the apoftle, that which thou foweft, is not quickened except it die. The intention of this anfwer is to teach us, that as the death and ferment of the grain fown in the ground, hinders not its rifing again; but is rather ab-folutely neceffary to its fpringing up in a plant: fo the death of the human body, is no hind-rance to it rifing again. *And that which thou foweft, thou foweft not that body that fhall be.*

This

This is to fhew us, that the body being
fown natural, and raifed fpiritual, is not the
fame in its refurrection, as it was in its
death; becaufe (as I have fhewn before) all
thofe qualities which conftituted the natural
character, are deftroyed in death : and the
fpiritual character as no longer reftrained, and
concealed by the former, is now perfectly fuftained in the refurrection. The body thus changed,
is faid, not to be the fame body; . that is,
the comparifon, which proves, that the fown
body, is not the fame as the rifen body; doth
not refpect its materiality, or identical exiftence,
but its *qualities*; or *mode* of exiftence only.

Where the apoftle faith, Thou foweft not
that body that fhall be, but bare grain, &c.
There are none fo fimple, I fuppofe, as to
imagine that the apoftle would not have us expect to reap wheat, where we fow wheat :
or that by another body, we are to expect *bar-
ley* where wheat is fown. Nay, his defign is
to fhew us, that though the grain fown be
bare, and fimple, yet it rifeth a glorious body,
producing many-fold : as an emblem of the
body, which is fown in corruption, but raifed
in glory; even an hundred fold, when compared with what it has in this life.

The grain which is fown, refpecting its fubftance, is not loft : for though it ferments and
dies, it fhoots upwards into the ftalk. Were
you *then* to take the ftalk properly out of the
earth, you fhall find that the fown grain, is faft
at the root in appearance : but upon examina-
tion, you may perceive, that all its fubftance,
every material particle, containing all its genuine

ine qualities are fpent; are rifen in the plant; and nothing remains but the chaff, or hufk, which is all of it that is loft. This is a fimile of the refurrection: All the original genuine properties of the body are preferved; and nothing loft but the chaff: *i. e.* the bafe qualities that adhered to it. *But God giveth it a body, as it hath pleafed him; and to every feed its own body.* The meaning of which, I apprehend to be, that God, without accounting for his ways to man, without their being able to comprehend the depths of his wifdom, and power, is pleafed in an ineffable manner, to give a body to the fown feed. Bewildered, and loft, in the refearches of reafon, we are conftrained to refolve all into the good pleafure of God. *God giveth it a body, as it hath pleafed him; and to every feed, its own body.* But if God does not give a human body, to every human body fown, how can every feed be faid to have its own body.

In the paffages above-cited, the apoftle is manifeftly fpeaking of the future refurrection of the body: but Mr. *Coppin*, and his admirers, will not fo underftand him. They will make it out in fuch a manner, as fays that the refurrection is paft. Thus erring concerning the truth, and overthrowing the faith of fome; in *The advancement of all things in Chrift*, &c. Chap. 6. he fpeaks thus, " God hath fowed the feed, " or planted the image of eternity, the image of " the divine Being, the image of himfelf, " which is *Jefus Chrift*, in this world, as in " general, fo particularly in *Adam* — in the " flefh of *Chrift*—in the flefh of his faints—

C "in

" in the whole world of things." What has
this unscriptural, this unmeaning proposition,
to do with the matter in hand? what hath
it to do with that scripture-passage, of which it
is a pretended exposition? what affinity has the
phraseology, or sense, (if it has any sense) of
his propositions, to this interrogation? *How are
the dead raised, and with what body do they
come?* And what relation doth it bear to the
apostle's answer, *Thou fool,* &c. except an as-
sertion of right, to appropriate the character?

The term, image; as applied to God, may be
understood in various senses. Kings, and ma-
gistrates, from their power and rule, may be
said to be the image of God. Any person,
exercising himself in works of mercy, com-
passion, love, benevolence, &c. may be said,
in so doing, to be an image of God.—The sun
is an image of his brightness; the rock of
his stability; the fire of his purity, &c. In
this sense, all creatures may be considered as
having somewhat of the divine image: The
heavens declare thy power, and firmament
sheweth forth thine handy work.

But, if by the image of God, we mean the
assemblage of all divine perfections; represented,
and reflected, as in a mirrour, which in the
scripture, is the primary sense of the term:
there is then, none other image of God, than
Jesus Christ: He is the brightness of the glory
of God, and the express image of his person.
The light of the knowledge of the glory of
God, is in the face of *Jesus Christ. Coppin* says,
that God planted this divine image in *Adam:*
but neither the prophets, nor apostles, say so.

Moses

Mofes indeed tells us, that God made man in his own image, and after his own likenefs. But this image, and likenefs of God, *in* whom, and *after* whom, man was made ; was *Jefus* *Chrift :* the fame yefterday, to-day, and forever.

God, eternal, invifible, immortal, incomprehenfible, was pleafed to exhibit an image of himfelf, of his own nature, and properties, in the perfon of his Son; who was with him, as one brought up with him from everlafting. By which medium he wrought all his works. And in which he was known, and his glories reflected on the angels, and on all the heavenly powers. In this image, and after his model and fimilitude (he being the head of mankind) was *Adam* formed. *Adam* was fo far from being the exprefs image of God in himfelf, or from having it planted, or fown in him ; that he, in his brighteft perfection and glory, was but an outward, fhadowy, fleeting figure, of him who is the perfect, exprefs, unchangeable, and eternal image of the invifible God.—Hence the apoftle calls *Adam* the figure of him that was to come.

Again, inftead of acknowledging *Chrift* himfelf to be the image of God, he talks of the image of God, being fown, or planted in the human nature of *Chrift* ; and that when *Chrift* laid down his flefh, by the death of the crofs, this image was raifed up into the divine nature, where it lives forever. Here he fhews himfelf to be a divider of *Chrift*, by diftinguifhing the *Chrift*, from the perfon of Jefus of *Nazareth*. In this he feems to follow *Cerinthus*, a perfon who lived in the firft century ; who held, that *Jefus* was the fon of *Jofeph* and *Mary*; but that

C 2.   *Chrift*

Chrift, in the form of a dove, defcended upon him
at his baptifm : and that when *Jefus* fuffered
death, *Chrift* flew up into heaven, without being
fenfible of any inconvenience. To confute the
errors of this heretic, and his followers, *John* is
reported to have wrote his gofpel. *Coppin* in his
definition of the true *Chrift* ; fays, he is to be in
us, to redeem and fave us as he was in the man
Chrift Jefus. He alfo fays, that when *Jefus* laid
down his flefh, by the death of the crofs, (the
Chrift, or) the image of God, was raifed up into
the divine nature, where it lives forever.

By faying that the image of God which *Chrift*
had in his human nature, was at his death,
raifed up into the divine nature, where it lives
forever: he affirms, either that the body, or
flefh of *Chrift*, did not rife again ; but that his
human nature perifhed and ceafed to be in
death : Or otherwife; that though his human
nature doth now exift, it is not the image of
God : nay, the image of God doth not fo much
as dwell in it *now*, according to him. But the
image of God is raifed up into the divine nature, where it lives forever. According to
which, there is no exhibited image of God now.
Thefe things are fo horribly blafphemous, and
antichriftian ; that they need neither the argument of reafon, nor fcripture, to confute them.

Again, what a rant it is, to talk of the image
of God being planted in the flefh of his faints!
and then to quote fundry paffages of fcripture,
in fupport thereof: which bear no more relation to *his* propofition, than they do to the *Coran*.

I have already fhewn from fcripture, experience, and reafon, that there is no fuch thing as
the

the divine image, or good principle dwelling in the individuals of mankind: neither in their flesh, nor spirit; and therefore shall say no more to it here.

Nor will I spend my time, to shew the impropriety of asserting, that this image is sown in the whole world of things; but shall leave the superlatively enlightned, to admire, and worship the divine image, in dogs, swine, serpents, &c. which are not creatures of the *smallest* consequence, in the whole world of things.

Thus, according to this author, the dead, or the seed sown, is *Jesus Christ*, or the divine image. And that this seed, was sown, died, and was buried, in the human nature, or flesh of man; and in the whole world of things. —That God raises this dead seed, or *Christ*, by his voice; And being risen in us, it returns to God again: whilst the nature and persons of men, with the whole world of things, are all left behind to perish. "Thus, (saith he) God hath "carried the image of himself, through all "things in the world, and to the end of all "things again even to himself." (And again) "This is the last and general resurrection."

Without doing him any injury, I may venture to affirm: that his doctrines are unscriptural, and unreasonable: tending to the subversion of christianity in general. For first, with *Hymeneus* and *Philetus*, he affirms, that the resurrection is past already. Secondly, he denies that the body rises at all. Thirdly, he denies that man, or any part of him, is the object of salvation. Fourthly, he asserts that the persons of men, having no pre-eminence above a beast, shall perish everlastingly as the beast.

Whether

Whether this man underftood the apoftles,. or payed any regard to their doctrine, or not, I leave the reader to judge : and fhall here ob- ferve, that if the matter in hand, had related only to the refurrection of *our bodies* ; I fhould not have meddled with it : but fhould have left *Coppin* and his admirers, to the time of the re- ftitution of all things ; when every man fhall be reftored to his right fenfes ; at leaft, fo far as to diftinguifh between truth and error. But the apoftle fhews us, that if the doctrine of the refurrection be not true, if there be no refur- rection of the dead, then *Chrift* is not raifed : and if he be not rifen, then our preaching is vain : our faith is vain : we are yet in our fins. Thus it appears to be, (not a meer opinion, a fpeculation, or fable ; but) a matter of the ut- moft importance : the fource, and evidence of our falvation : our happinefs in time and in eternity.

Again, this author, denies the human nature of *Chrift*, No. 2. page 26. where he fcoffs at a corporal *Chrift :* and No. 3. page 58, 59. where he more than once, treats the doctrine of our Saviour's having a body of flefh and bones, with fneers and derifion : as alfo in fundry parts of his book, intitled, *The advancement of all things in Chrift*, &c. How amazing ! that any perfon who believes, or even pretends to believe the fcriptures, fhould difpute the truth of our Saviour's having a body of flefh and bones : when the evangelifts affure us, that the Lord *Jefus*, after his refurrection, was particu- larly careful, to give his difciples the fulleft evidence, the moft indifputable proof, of his
being

being rifen; in the very fame body wherein he
fuffered and died.

Of the truth of this, he convinced their eyes,
their ears, their hands, and heart.—He who
knew all things, forefaw that men of perverfe
minds would arife: who, (though they confef-
fed themfelves chriftians) would conteft, and
deny, the reality of his refurrection. His form,
his features, his voice, his wounds, the materiality of his flefh and bones; all which were
manifeft, and proved to a demonftration; perfectly convinced his difciples, that the fame, individual, material body of *Jefus*, which was
crucified, died, and was buried, was rifen from
the dead; nor was it poffible for them to be
deceived, by any phantom or fhadowy appearance; becaufe he convinced them of his having flefh, and bones; which they very well
knew, were not the properties of a fpirit.

Behold my hands, and my feet, (faith our Saviour) *that it is I myfelf: handle me, and fee, for
a fpirit hath not flefh and bones, as ye fee me have.*
And again to *Thomas, Reach hither thy finger,
and behold my hands, and reach hither thy hand,
and thruft it into my fide : and be not faithlefs, but
believing.* But the *Chrift,* whom *Coppin,* and
his admirers reverence, neither is, nor was capable of making any fuch propofal to his followers; becaufe he has no body of flefh and
bones; nor indeed has he any other exiftence,
than in their antichriftian conceit.

That the *Chrift* whom the apoftles preached,
had a body of flefh and bones, is manifeft:
where *Paul* tells the church, that they are *members of his body, of his flefh,—and of his bones.*

But

But this propofition, cannot poffibly be true, if *Chrift* has no body of flefh and bones ; as this author afferts. Let God be true, and every man a liar. The word of truth affures us, that he has a body of flefh and bones ; and that this body, notwithftanding all its wounds and bruifes, was fo preferved that not a bone thereof was broken. But it was preferved to no purpofe, if it did not rife again : or, if it was loft afterwards.—The Holy Ghoft, bearing witnefs of the Lord *Jefus*, by the prophets ; teftifies, that a bone of him fhould not be broken. Speaking of the paffover, the type of *Chrift* ; he fays, *Neither fhall ye break a bone thereof*, Exod. xii. 46. And again, *nor break any bone of it*, Num. ix. 12. And again, *He keepeth all his bones : not one of them is broken*, Pfal. xxxiv. 20. And, that this related to the body of the Lord *Jefus*, the evangelift *John* bare witnefs. Our Saviour, and thofe who fuffered with him, being crucified on the eve of an high fabbath among the Jews ; the latter befought *Pilate* (as the crucified were long dying) that they might have leave to break their legs : and to take them down, that their bodies might not be feen on their croffes on the following day : To this he confented ; upon which, they brake the legs of thofe who were crucified with our Lord ; but when they came to *Jefus*, and faw that he was already dead, they brake not his legs. And the beloved difciple in his remarks upon this, fays, *for thefe things were done that the fcripture fhould be fulfilled, A bone of him fhall not be broken*, John xix. 36, Thus, the apoftle fhews that it was not accident, but the

the purpofe and council of God, that defeated the defign of the *Jews:* when they would have broken his legs with the others. Nor are we to refpect it as a trifling, or common occurrence: That would be to impeach the wifdom of God, who had fo long before his fufferings, declared by his prophets, that a bone of him fhould not be broke

The prefervation of our Saviour's body was for his own glory, and for the benefit and advantage of mankind. As mankind were comprehended in his body, flefh of his flefh, and bone of his bone ; it denoted their final prefervation and fecurity in the fame body : Not the fmalleft member, was to be feparated from the whole ; nor the body from the head : that we might live by him. It alfo denoted his faithfulnefs, power, and love, in preferving the whole body, all that had been committed to his truft.

Again, Mr. *Richard Coppin* by propofing *Chrift* to be a meer quality in man, denies his perfon, No. 1. page 13. He fays that *Chrift* "is to " be in you to teach, redeem, and fave you, " as he was in the man *Chrift Jefus.*" Thus according to him, the man *Chrift Jefus,* who was born at *Bethlehem* of a pure virgin, who wrought many miracles, and went about doing good ; who fuffered, and died upon a crofs, in the reign of *Tiberias Cæfar* ; and who rofe again from the dead, on the third day ; I fay, according to *Coppin,* this perfon was not the *Chrift,* in fpirit, and truth : but that the true *Chrift* was in him only, to redeem, and fave
him ;

him ; in like manner as he is to be in the people.

And No. 3. pag. 59. he fays : " And you fay,
" When Chrift, who is our life, fhall appear ;
" then fhall we alfo appear with him in glory :
" and this life, even Chrift, you fay is eternal
" life. Then I anfwer, this muft not be meant
" of a body of flefh, and bones, for that can-
" not be our eternal life. And this life, the
" apoftles then waited for, and received ; which
" was a fpiritual Chrift, even Chrift in them
" the hope of glory : and not a flefhly perfonal
" Chrift as you fay ; for how can fuch a one be
" in us to be our eternal life ?"

If I miftake not, Mr. *Coppin* intitles his
works, [in defence of which, that which now is
a 're-publifhing in numbers, was written :] *A
Blow at the Serpent.* But whether his admirers
will excufe me or not, I am obliged to give it a
new title ; and as I think a very juft one ; *i. e.* A
BLOW AT THE SEED OF THE
WOMAN.

He fays, that Chrift as a perfon, or as having
a body of flefh, and bones, cannot be our eternal life. That our Saviour hath a body of flefh,
and bones, I have already proved from the
fcriptures. And I fhall now endeavour to prove,
that the perfon of Chrift, as having fuch a body, is our eternal life.

Our Saviour, in the 6th of *John*; declares
that his flefh is meat indeed, and that his blood
is drink indeed. And faith, whofo eateth my
flefh, and drinketh my blood, hath eternal life.
But how can we eat or drink what hath no exiftence ? can a man fill his belly with the eaft
wind ?

wind ? can he drink of a river, whofe waters are
cut off, and whofe ftreams are perfectly dried
up ? We anfwer, he cannot. It is not meerly faying to the body, be fed, that feeds it:
nor, will our bidding it be warm, adminifter
any heat to it.

As the Lord *Jefus*, has propofed to all gene-
rations, that fuch who eat his flefh, and drink
his blood, hath eternal life ; fhall live thereby,
&c. I think I may venture to propofe, with
as much confidence, and upon much better
grounds than *Coppin* afferts the contrary : that
our Saviour always has a body, a material body,
a body of flefh and bones. And that this body, as united with his foul, to the deity; in the
glorious perfon of Immanuel, is the eternal life :
Hence whofo eateth him, fhall live by him.

To eat and to drink his flefh and blood, certainly intends fuch an apprehenfion of our
union and onenefs with Chrift; as infpires us
with wifdom, refolution, and power to appropriate him. So to mingle with his flefh and
blood; *i. e.* his human nature ; that all his labours, fufferings, victories, and triumphs, being
ours as they are his ; we might eat his flefh,
and drink his blood : that is derive life, purity,
confidence, and blifs; from our being one flefh
and blood with him; intitling us to his peace
and joy, which is unfpeakable, and full of
glory.

What a perfon eats and drinks, being properly digefted in the ftomach; the nutritive part,
after chylification, becomes blood ; and ming-
les with the whole mafs : adding health,
ftrength, and magnitude to the body through-
out.

out. Thus, what a perfon eats and drinks, becomes one with himfelf : and except it does fo,
the perfon is not nourifhed, nor can he live
thereby.

In like manner, to eat the fiefh, and drink
the blood of the Son of man ; is to apprehend
our union with him, our memberfhip in his
body, even of his flefh and of his bones : in
fuch fort, that becoming one with his flefh and
blood, we rejoice together with him ; in all the
benefits of his humiliation, and exaltation in the
body. And thus, that *Chrift* who hath a body
of flefh and bones, is our eternal life.

As *Coppin* tauntingly afks, how a perfonal
Chrift can be faid to be in us, as our eternal
life? I anfwer, Chrift, in the fcriptures, is faid
to be our eternal life, in a two-fold fenfe ;. firft,
as he hath taken upon him the feed of *Abraham,*
perfonating, and wearing the people in the body
of his flefh : he was born in them, circumcifed in
them, baptized in them, tempted in them, fulfilled all righteoufnefs in them ; he fuffered in them,
died in them, rofe again in them, afcended in them,
and liveth forever in them. Thus faith the prophet : *Lord, thou wilt ordain peace for us : for thou
alfo haft wrought all our works in us.* And thus
is *Chrift* in us, the hope of glory. Thus did
Job behold God in his flefh. Thus all the
promifes, relative to God's dwelling in the people, to his coming in the flefh, *&c.* are fulfil-
ed in him. In *Chrift Jefus,* all the promifes
are yea and amen. Here we underftand, how
the perfonal *Chrift* is in us, and is our eternal
life, and hope of glory. The life which he
lives, in his own perfon, he lives *in* us, and *for*
us :

us: Hence the apostle tells us, that the eternal life which God hath given us, is in his Son. And our Saviour says, *Because I live, you shall live also.*

Again, *Christ* is said to be in man by faith, by revelation, by manifestation, by his spirit, &c. In this sense, he is in us, according to our individual persons. Faith is the evidence of things unseen, &c. Therefore it is that witness; *in*, and *with* power, light, and love to our minds; of the glorious person, and salvation of *Christ*: Though we have not seen him, neither are we permitted to determine of him by what we feel, or know from ourselves; yet our understandings are enlightened to discern him, according to truth: our wills consent to his salvation, and submit to his glory: our affections rejoice in him: our conscience hath peace, purity, and perfection in him.

The *Christ*, thus explained to our judgment, thus glorious before the eyes of our mind, thus borne witness of in our hearts, by the Spirit of truth; is not some creature of fancy, or the offspring of enthusiasm: but a personal *Christ*; that very *Jesus* whom the apostles preached; that identical person who died upon the cross, without the gates of *Jerusalem*: who rose from the dead, who ascended up on high, and who liveth forever. This person, according to his personal properties, glory, grace, and salvation; being explained, revealed, and witnessed of, in, and unto our faculties, is *Christ*, dwelling in our hearts by faith: There, realized (though unseen) in his person, and benefits: dwelling there, as the object of our peace and purity.   *Coppin*

Coppin cannot conceive how a perfonal *Chrift*
can be faid to dwell in our hearts, no more
than the *Jews* could conceive, how he could
give them his flefh to eat : but this is certainly
owing to his ignorance, both of the fcriptures,
and of the power of God : Where he has not a
mind to believe any thing, he exercifes his reafonings, afking, how can a perfonal Chrift be
in us ? He might as well have afked, how can
the body, when dead, and mouldered to duft,
ever rife again ? how could the body of *Chrift*
afcend in air ; without fteps, or fome other con-
venience to go up by, *&c. &c. ?* For thefe are
matters which he pofitively denies, becaufe he
cannot comprehend them : But with regard to
his own fyftem, he is as far above all *reafon* in
his propofitions, as the heavens are above the
earth : he is there, all infpiration, and infallibility : trampling the weak and beggarly elements
of reafon, and common fenfe, under his feet.

I hope, I have fufficiently proved, that our
Saviour hath a material body ; a body of flefh
and bones : and have alfo fhewn, how he, as
having fuch a body, may be faid to be in us,
as our eternal life. I would here obferve of
Coppin, and his admirers, that *their* Chrift is *no
body* : They will neither allow him to have a
human body ; nor to be a perfon. Confequently, he is neither God nor man : nor is he
a fpirit of any kind ; otherwife he muft be
perfonal. *Chrift*, is by them, fuppofed to be a
principle, or quality of good : originally im-
planted in every creature. This fuppofed good,
he calls the *Jacob*, which is loved of God : the
left precious ; the believer : the *Chrift, &c.*
And

And the evil principle, or quality in man, he calls the *Esau*, which God hates; the repro- bate, the unbeliever, the antichrist, *&c.*

If you compare the above, with the doc- trines of the *Manichees*; you will soon perceive that *Coppin*'s sentiments, are only a revival of the *Manicheean* herefy. They held that there were two principles; the one of good, from which proceeded the good soul of man; and the other of evil, from which proceeded the bad soul, with the body; and all other corporeal, and perishable creatures. They, also held that the good soul, went to God, unto whom it was rejoined. They denied the refurrection of the body. They denied that *Chrift* had a real body.—Whether *Coppin* gleaned his sentiments in the *Manicheean* field, or whether they were sown in him by the fame hand which firft fow- ed them in *Manes*, the leader of the fect; I shall not determine: But manifeft it is, that they are perfectly fimilar; and that they raife the fame inferences from them.

Hence it is, that in No. 2. page 45. he says " Man is become one with God, in all that " God was above man."—I hope I shall be able to cloath my ideas, properly; and if I am, I doubt not but to detect, and expofe, the fal- lacy, and danger, of this blafphemous propo- fition. He pretends that this propofition fol- lows of confequence, from man's reconciliation in *Chrift*, to the Father: and thus denies the perfonality, pre-eminence, and medium of *Chrift*. Excufe me, if I fubjoin part of a letter, which I wrote to a perfon in the country, not long fince, on a fimilar fubject.

" I

" I cannot but greatly diflike that propofition in your letter, *of our being equal with God.* It is faid of our Saviour, indeed; that *he thought it no robbery to be equal with God.* This was intended as a proof of his real godhead : fince in a ftrict fenfe of the word, God has no equal. Whatever equality, our Saviour as a man, has to God ; it is according to that grace, and favour only, which the deity hath conferred upon the human nature in his perfon. Hence he is called the man, God's fellow. That is, his companion, his friend, whom he hath exalted at his own right hand, to be a prince, and a Saviour : And unto whom he is fo clofely, myfterioufly, and eternally united ; that the Lord *Jefus,* according to the properties of his human nature, ftands invefted by the godhead, with all divine perfections : fo that it was no robbery for *him* to think himfelf equal with God. But it does not follow from thence, that *we* are equal with God : It is manifeft robbery, for *us* to think in fuch a manner : we rob the fcriptures of their truth ; for they declare the contrary : We rob that God of his honour ; who fays, my glory I will not give to another : We rob our Lord *Jefus Chrift* of his pre-eminence, and are fchifmatics in the firft fenfe of the word. It is, as if the foot fhould fay, I am the head ; therefore put the crown upon me ; or at leaft, let me have a crown, as well as the head. If we claim a right to fay, that we are equal with God ; becaufe *Chrift* is equal with him : Is it not as if the foot fhould fay, I muft needs be the feat of wifdom to the body ; becaufe the head is fuch ? Or, I muft needs

have

have the pre-eminence and crown, becaufe the head hath them? do not you perceive how groundlefs, and falfe, all fuch inferences are?

To infer that we are equal with God; becaufe *Chrift* thought it no robbery to be equal with God; is either to deny, that *Chrift* is any other perfon than the church, and, that the fcriptures have any other meaning than the people; in what they fpeak of him: Or, if we confefs him to be an individual, a diftinct perfon, wholly independent of mankind, in point of exiftence: I fay, if we thus confefs him, and yet infift on our being equal with God; becaufe he is fo: we certainly rob him of his preeminence, and deny him as the mediator between God and man. To fay, that *Chrift* hath none other body, or perfon, than the people; is the fame in argument, as if we faid, the head hath none other reality of exiftence, than what it hath in the hand, or in the foot.

The Lord *Jefus*, in his perfon, and in the myftery of his body, may be confidered as fimple, and aggregate. Simple, as he ftands alone, in an uncompounded exiftence; where he is not the people, neither are the people him. In this point of view, he ftands high above every creature in heaven, on earth, and under the earth; he is *there* fairer than the fons of men, and the perpetual object of their worfhip.

But in his office-capacity, as he reprefented, and perfonated mankind; which he did in his birth, obedience, fufferings, death, refurrection, and afcenfion; and now doth in his everlafting life; he was the aggregate. He was in all *this*, the fum total of mankind; who were thus gathered

D into

into one body. But the aggregate, was fubject to the fimple. Hence it is, that the people,
who are purified, and exalted in the aggregate;
pay eternal homage to the fimple; falling before his feet, and forever finging, Worthy is the
Lamb, &c. And whilft they acknowledge him
to be the Lord, to be the only holy, they confefs that the fimple is the head of the aggregate.

The apoftle tells us, that the head of every
man is *Chrift*, and the head of *Chrift* is God.
From this, you may perceive, that we have no
immediate *union* with God; much lefs an e-
quality with him.

It is *Chrift* only, in his fimple exiftence;
who is united to God : he only, is one with the
Father : In him, the deity is immediate
head to the human nature : which branch of
human nature, in the man *Chrift Jefus*, is immediately head over all things, to the aggregate;
i. e. to his body the church.

By *Chrift*, as the medium between God, and
man; every good, and perfect gift cometh.
He is the immediate receiver of all good, from
God. He is the exalted, he is the anointed,
he is the crowned King of kings, and Lord of
lords : whilft we, without envy, without re-
pining, rejoice in his glory; and are joyfully
fubject to him.

Should it be granted, that the hand, the
foot, or the more uncomely parts of the body;
have a right to claim an equality with the
head, (which is not an unexceptionable rule)
yet this right, in every member, muft be
limited to its own head. With what propriety
then

then can we claim an equality with God, who is the head of *Chrift*, and not our immediate head?

We certainly can claim no more, than to be as our own head; nor is that claim afcertained any farther, than as he is confidered the aggre-gate: for in his fimple, and individual exift-ence, he is anointed with the oil of gladnefs a-bove his fellows. He is *there* the object of our worfhip, love, praife, delight, and eternal ad-miration.

From all which, I conclude, that the propo-fition of our being equal with God, is meer rant; and more than bordering upon blafphe-my. It is productive of many hurtful and per-nicious errors : it infpires mankind with lucife-rian pride; though in comparifon of the Al-mighty, they are lighter than vanity, they are lefs than nothing. It difhonours our Creator, by making him fuch a one as ourfelves. It de-ftroys the medium between God and man; which is *Chrift Jefus* the Lord. It denies the *pre-eminence* of our Saviour, as head over all things to his body the church.

But as Mr. *Richard Coppin*, in his writings, does not gather with *Chrift*; as he denies the body, and perfon of the Lord *Jefus:* it will be objected probably, that my arguments do not comprehend the grounds of his propofition. I believe I am as well aware of his meaning, as his admirers are; excepting none of them. But I con-fefs, there is fome difficulty, in framing argu-ments againft things which will *fcarcely* bear any : as is the cafe here. He fays that "Man is be-"come one with God, in all that God was above

"man."

" man." But it is neither true in divinity, nor
philofophy. Is man become one with God in
his eternity, wifdom, power, purity, &c. &c.?
the propofition is odious, and blafphemous.

Had he faid of *Chrift*, according to the properties of his *human nature*; that he is become
one with God, in all that God was above him;
he had erred againft the truth. But, as he denies the perfon of *Chrift*; he muft by *man*,
whom he fays is one with God, mean the creature, himfelf, his brethren, &c. And does it
appear, either to men, or angels; that man, a
worm, fubject to paffions, and compaffed a-
bout with infirmities, is one with God; in all
the tremendous height of his glory and majef-
ty? Nay, as the heavens are above the earth,
fo are his ways, and his thoughts above ours.

Again, as he denies the perfonality of *Chrift*—
as he treats all the fcripture-account of things
allegorically.—as he fays, that the believer, and
unbeliever, are, in every man, &c. He acts
confiftent with himfelf, in making out that falvation, [which our Saviour taking upon him
the feed of *Abraham* by his obedience, fufferings, death and refurrection, wrought out for
us in his own perfon:] to confift in a work, or
operation, wrought within us.

" God (faith he) reveals all his fecrets
" within, and all the works that he doth in
" this new creation, he doth within us: And
" therefore, let all thofe that defire to be
" made partakers of this new creation, look
" for it within them; for there will God
" work it." *Advancement of all things in Chrift*,
&c. pag. 24.

God,

God, who at fundry times, and in divers manners, fpake unto our fathers by the prophets, faid, *Be ye glad, and rejoice in that which I create.* But if this new creation is wrought in us; it follows that we are to rejoice in ourfelves. But the apoftle tells us, that *Chrift* is made of God unto us wifdom, righteoufnefs, fanctification, and redemption; that whofoever glorieth, fhould glory in the Lord. *Chrift* fays, *Look unto me all ye ends of the earth, and be ye faved:* but *Coppin* fays, we muft look unto ourfelves for it. The apoftle fays, We *are God's workmanfhip created anew in Chrift Jefus,* &c. But *Coppin* fays, we are created anew in ourfelves. The promife, which God made, of creating all things anew; *Coppin* fays he fulfills, by working it within us. But *Chrift* told the apoftle *John,* that this promife was fulfilled in *his* perfon; *It is done, faith he, I am the Alpha, and Omega, the beginning and the end.* The prophet fpeaking of mankind, (not excepting Mr. *Coppin*) fays, *The beft of them is as a briar, the moft upright is fharper than a thorn hedge,* &c. &c. *therefore will I look unto the Lord,* &c. The apoftle fpeaks of the fentence of condemnation in ourfelves, that we fhould not truft in ourfelves, but in the living God.

If we try it by experience, reafon, and common fenfe, this new creation is not difcernable in man. There has no phyfical change paffed over him; his body is the fame, fubject to pain, ficknefs, and death; and compaffed about with manifold infirmities. Nor is there any inward change, anfwerable to a new creation: where old things are done away, and all things are

becom:

become new. Thofe who pretend to the high-eft refinements, and fpirituality, are men fub-ject to like paffions with others; as is very obvious in the author himfelf, who could not bear the leaft oppofition from his antago-nifts. Their cenfures, and reflections, wounded his vanity, and felf-importance, in fuch fort that he could not contain himfelf; but refolving not to be behind hand with them, he gave them as good as they fent; yea, I think rather exceeded them in the article of judgment and cenfure. But this I fuppofe he thought he had a right to do, as being more fpiritual than his opponents. And I have fufficient reafon to conclude, that the cafe is ftill the fame, with fome of his admirers.

And if men are cenforious, proud, vain, and felfifh, with what propriety, or juftice, can they look for this new creation in themfelves? and wherein doth it confift? If its a truth, that they love God, it is an invifible one. But it is a truth vifible enough that they love the prefent world; and yet the apoftle faith, *If the love of the world is in any man, the love of the Father is not in him.* They may tell us that they love their brethren, but it is a matter that we are no further fure of, then as we take their bare word for it; but this, we are very fure of, that they love themfelves; that being notorious enough. And yet to be lovers of their own felves, is ranked by the apoftle among the re-probate characters.

In fact, where men differ nothing from others; (except in partiallity to themfelves) opi-nion, fentiment, or theory, is not fufficient to

prove

prove them spiritual men, or that the new creation is within them.

Pray, is not this enthufiaftic conceit, this
vain-glorious imagination, or the good principle in man; the beaft, *that was, and is not?*
that it is full of the names of blafphemy, I
think is plain enough : for, it arrogates the perfonal characters, names, works, fufferings,
death, refurrection, afcenfion and glory; of our
only Lord and God, *Jefus Chrift*; ufurps his
crown, and throne; and exalts itfelf againft
all that is called God, and that is to be wor-
fhipped.

This is the beaft that all the world worfhip-
peth, and goeth after. Pagans, Mahometans,
Jews, Chriftians of all denominations, and of
every fect, worfhip this beaft; going after him per-
petually, in their admiration, defires, and efteem.

This beaft, bears different names, according
to the different languages of men : The Heathen call him virtue. The Jews, and Mahometans, call him obedience : only the one refpect
Mofes, (as their prophet and legiflator) and the
other, *Mahomet*. Amongft Chriftians, this beaft
bears divers names, according to their various
divifions; and every diftinct name, by which it
is called, may be confidered as the fhibboleth of
the fect, making ufe of it. By fome he is called
grace, and the falvation of man, very cordially im-
puted to him; to the difhonour of the Son of God.

By others, he is called inward holinefs, fanctification, imparted righteoufnefs, inherent
righteoufnefs, &c. Whilft others, call him the
inward light, the Spirit, &c: and make him
infallible in reproof, inftruction, and doctrine.

And

[56]

And again, there are others, as *Coppin*, &c. who call him *Chrift*, the elect, the believer, yea, God himfelf.

Now I fay, .that the different names, and epithets, made ufe of amongft all thefe ; (notwithftanding their various attachment to men and things) makes no difference at all, with refpect to their object of admiration, and worfhip, or to their hope of falvation : for the terms, virtue, obedience, grace, holinefs, light, or *Chrift* as fuppofed to be naturally in man, are all congenial; and characteriftics of the beaft *that was, and is not:* And this beaft is always manifeft, from its being oppofed to the perfon of *Jefus Chrift* our Lord : and to that free, and gracious falvation which he has wrought out for mankind, without works of righteoufnefs ; as done by them.

As to the *origin* of; this fuppofed good in man, its admirers are not perfectly agreed about it : there are fome, fuch as *Coppin*, &c. who confider it as the feed of God, fown in man at his firft creation ; which was not totally loft, or extinguifhed by the fall ; but buried only, as it were, under a heap of rubbifh : from whence, not being quite dead, it fends forth, fome weak breathings by way of conviction, repentance, defire, &c. until it hear the voice of God, and come forth out of its grave. But others reject this, as unfcriptural, unwarrantable, and enthufiaftic ; and tell us, that this good is only to be attained by ftudy, by induftry, by obferving and copying good examples, &c. Others, tell us, that it proceeds from the impreffions which the belief of particular doctrines makes upon the mind.

mind. And others, that it is the free gift of God to them, without any confideration whatever. Thofe divers opinions, caufe difputes, and bickerings, even amongft fuch who are otherwife perfectly agreed in patronizing the fame matter.

But in the general, it is enough; to be orthodox in this particular. To profefs it, to make pretenfions (at leaft) of being poffeffed of it, to converfe much of it, to declaim in its favour, to paint out its beauties, &c. *this*, in general, I fay, is thought fufficient to denominate a man virtuous and good. But if he add to this, an appearance of care and diligence, in cultivating it; by practifing fome aufterities, relative to meats, drinks, reft, fleep, and things of that nature; if his apparel, gefture, fpeech, and manner, bear any, even the leaft correfpondence with his pretenfion, it is then enough *indeed*: it makes no difference, whether he believes in God, and in *Chrift*, or not: and though he may have many lufts, and vices predominant in him; fuch as pride, incontinence, covetoufnefs, deceitfulnefs, cruelty, fuperftition, &c. yet thefe, if known, are in the eftimation of mankind, abundantly over-ballanced by the fuppofed good which is in them: though the latter, in reality, can only be in *appearance*, whereas the former is *manifeft*.

Upon this principle it is, that numbers among the Chriftians, both antient and modern, have thought it right to compliment the Heathen, fuch as *Socrates, Cicero, Seneca*, and others, with the favour and falvation of their God: and that not becaufe they were human creatures,

creatures, or the offspring of *Adam*; but because they were great men! good men! wife
men! they said a great many wife and good
things. Their admirers among the Christians,
in order to make them speak some knowledge of
the true God, and of *Christ*; stretch their say-
ings upon the tenter-hooks of their enthusia-
ftic fancy, in such fort, that they break their
connection, and render their fine things quite
unmeaning.

Thus the relator of *Anson's* voyage, &c.
tells us, how that a jesuit, (in favour of Mr.
Anson) explained that article of the Romish
church, which denies the falvation of he-
retics; in a lax and hypothetical fenfe: Wherefore? why truly, on the account of fome fuppofed goodnefs in him: he did not ravifh their
women; nor kill and eat their men; that fell
into his power: though it was not their perfons, but their gold, that he was in fearch of:
In the taking of which from them; neither his
modefty, as a philofopher, nor his felf-denial,
as a chriftian, was fo very confpicuous, as to encourage them to canonize him. But conftitu-
tion, or accident, (befriending him in fome o-
ther particulars) gained him the reputation of a
faint (in thofe parts) it feems.

But

It is faid of the grand vizior *Cuprogli*, that when dying;
fome of the laft words that he fpake, fixing his eyes upon
the Alcoran, were thefe: "Prophet, I fhall foon fee whe-
"ther thy words are true; but be they true or falfe, I am
"fure of being happy, if virtue be the beft of all reli-
"gions" He was certainly a perfon of much fagacity;
courageous, and faithful to his mafter: But if this is virtue,
it

[59]

But a perfect, uniform practice, is not at all neceſſary to the formation of this character; to be a zealous theoriſt is ſufficient: with ſome ſpecious appearances of virtue; however irregular, or tarniſhed with pride, ſelf-ſeeking, &c. Thus a perſon of this character, ſhall be judged to have a ſure title to happineſs: whether he believe in God, in *Chriſt*, in *Moſes*, or in *Mahomet*; or indeed if he believe in neither. Diametrically oppoſite to truth, as reſting upon reaſon and experience: and in the moſt glaring contradiction to divine revelation: it is aſſerted upon this principle, that every truly happy man, is wholly the ſon of his own actions: without being under the leaſt obligation to the grace, mercy, and love of his God and Redeemer.

Mankind in the general, make this their fundamental, whilſt matters of faith, are conſidered, rather as a ſcience to be ſtudied: or as ſomewhat calculated for men to employ their wits about. Thus, whatever they profeſs to believe; in every time of danger, their corpſe of reſerve is their own goodneſs.

I call

---

it is not impoſſible to find a virtuous dog. This man, ſo virtuous in his own eyes, was, to all appearance, a ſtranger to humanity, to the univerſal love of mankind, and to that ſelf-denial, &c. which conſtitute true virtue. He was proud, cunning, and cruel; but aſſiduous in his office: and an inſtrument perfectly qualified to raiſe the pride and pomp of a tyrant, in the deſtruction of thouſands of his fellow-creatures. And yet this is the perſon, who, in the article of death (when he can do no more miſchief) ſings a requiem to his ſoul, becauſe virtue is the beſt of all religions.

I call this the beaft, becaufe I think, it an-fwers to the character of that beaft fpoken of in the book of the Revelations, whom all the world goeth after: the character is there drawn up very brief; *i. e.* WHICH WAS, AND IS NOT. By which, I fuppofe, we may under-ftand; that there was once, before the fall of *Adam*, fome truth, in what man now vainly, and falfly pretends to. Therefore, that which *was, is not:* it hath now, none other exiftence in man, than what it has in pride and igno-rance.

Upon this beaft, rides the great whore, or the falfe church, compofed as I have fhewn, of all nations, kindreds and tongues; and of all profeffions.

And yet, notwithftanding there is fuch an admiring multitude, fuch a cloud of witneffes daily chaunting forth the praifes of this beaft: The moft curious fearcher, can never find out, by reafon and fcripture, (nor by reafon alone, confiftent with its ideas of the divine perfec-tions) this boafted good, this divine ftamina in man: nor can the moft intelligible fpeaker de-fcribe it, as exifting in the creature, in any de-gree of confiftency, with what is notorious, de-monftrable and certain in him.

Nay, God himfelf, (whofe eyes are as flames of fire, and whofe eyelids try the heart of the children of men) cannot find out this good in man: he fays, that he *looked down from hea-ven upon the children of men, to fee if there were any that did underftand, that did feek God: every one of them is gone back; they are altogether become filthy; there is none that doth good, no not one,*

Pf.

Pf. liii. 2, 3. and xiv. 2, 3. God, upon examining the human heart, tells us, that every imagination of the thoughts of man's heart, is evil and that continually ; and that the heart, is defperately wicked and deceitful above all things. And again, that the good man is perifhed out of the earth ; there is none upright amongft men : the beft of them is as a briar ; and the moft upright, is fharper than a thorn hedge. Our Saviour and his apoftles, teftify that this good is not in man. Our bleffed Lord, though holy, harmlefs, undefiled, would not fuffer them to give *him* the epithet of good, whilft they faw him only as man, faying, Why calleft thou me good ? *there is none good but one, even God.* And the apoftles faith, if any man hath whereof he may glory in the flefh, I more. Yet he counts it all but lofs, for the excellency of the knowledge of *Chrift Jefus* his Lord ; yea, but dung, that he might win *Chrift*, and be found in him. How vain and frivolous then, are all the pretenfions of men, to this new creation, falvation, or holinefs as wrought in them.

Again, Mr. *Coppin* fays, with a great degree of boldnefs, and certainty ; that all mankind fhall be faved, No. 1. ch. 6. Hence, I can account for the attachments of particular people, to his writings : for had he been a profeffed Infidel, with refpect to faith in *Chrift*, this very opinion, of univerfal falvation, would fufficiently recommend him to thofe who have nothing befides to comfort their minds with ; which, it is to be feared, is the cafe with too many of fuch who make a point of it.

But

But in this, the author is ſtrangely incon-
ſiſtent: for his hypotheſis is, that ſalvation,
the *new creation*, &c. is wrought in the creature; and that every man is to look for it in
himſelf. But it remains to be proved, that
this new creation, this ſalvation, is wrought in
every man: And yet, except it be thus
wrought within them, they cannot be ſaved,
according to him: But the apoſtle ſays, All
men have not faith. And as the terms faith,
Chriſt, ſalvation, &c. are ſynonimous with Mr.
Coppin; either he, or the apoſtle, are in the
wrong, if he ſay, that this ſalvation is in every
man: For my own part, I ſhall, for ſome
weighty reaſons, always give the preference to
the apoſtle.

Had he aſſerted the ſalvation of all mankind,
upon the principle of *Chriſt*; through what he
has done, and ſuffered for them in his own
perſon; it would at leaſt have had a more
plauſible, and conſiſtent appearance: but to aſſert it upon the following principles, which
are his: " Let all thoſe who deſire to be made
" partakers of this new creation, look for it
" within them, for there God will work it."
And again, " Not to look for the riſing of a
" fleſhly body, but a ſpiritual body within,
" for the truth of all things is within." I ſay,
to aſſert univerſal ſalvation upon thoſe principles, ſo very repugnant to the ſcriptures, and
to common ſenſe, was a moſt unadviſed conceit. If every man is to judge of his future
and eternal ſtate, by thoſe inward and divine
appearances; and not according to the love of
God, manifeſt through the ſufferings, death,

and

and refurrection of the Lord *Jefus:* there are but few, nay there are none, who will have a juft and clear title to it.

But alas, we are only upon the furface as yet, we have not founded the depths of this author.—In the firft chapter of this book, in-titled, *The advancement of all things in Chrift* ; he tells us, that he had obferved amongft pro-feffors, people of oppofite fentiments; the one part holding, that all mankind fhould be faved ; and the other afferting, that a part only fhould be faved : Upon which . Mr. *Coppin* fays, " There is a miftake in both thefe parties, nei-" ther of them underftanding the mind of God, " nor the myftery of his will, as laid down in " a dead letter. *" A moft furprizing decla-ration

---

* It is a very pernicious error, to call the fcripture a dead letter: for our Saviour faith, *The words that I fpeak unto you, they are fpirit and they are life.* By which words, he means, thofe which the evangelifts penn'd from his mouth : As alfo thofe which he, in the Spirit of truth, put into the mouths of his apoftles. Again, to confider the fcriptures as a dead letter, is to deny them as a rule for the trial of fpirits : which is to give all private fpirits an opportunity to affert their being of God : however incon-fiftent and contrary to each other. Again, If the writings of the apoftles be a dead letter : then, every man fuppo-fing himfelf to be led by the Spirit, is at liberty, not only to put what conftruction he pleafes upon their doctrines ; but alfo to correct them, and contradict them, where they do not fuit him. Hence, may be eafily difcerned, what diforder and confufion muft neceffarily follow the propofition that the fcriptures are a dead letter. It is not of the fcriptures, that the apoftle fpeaks where he fays *the letter killeth.* Nor is it of that fpirit, by which any man profeffes to be led, and inftructed, in a manner independent of the fcriptures : that he fpeaks, where he fays *the Spirit giveth life.* It is the meer coinage

ration indeed! neither the whole of mankind,
nor a part of them are to be faved! I fhould
have thought, that the moft fimple, and un-
biaffed mind upon earth, would have readily
concluded, that the one or the other was in the
right: that where there was a falvation of mankind, either the whole, or a part of them
would be faved, though they might not determine

---

coinage of an antichriftian brain to call the fcriptures a dead
letter: and as foreign from the defign of the apoftle, as light
is from darknefs. The apoftle, by the letter underftands the
law of commandments contained in ordinances; which, by
reafon of their darknefs and contrariety unto us, are a dead
and killing letter. And by the Spirit, he intends the Lord
Jefus, the fubftance, and fulnefs of all grace, fignified by the
ordinances; who having abolifhed them in himfelf, as being
the end of the law, is called the Spirit which giveth life. The
law confifts of precepts, requifites and threatnings: and the
depravity of human nature, being fuch; that mankind are
utterly incapable of fulfilling the precept, of producing the
requifite, or of enduring the punifhment, they are, in point
of confolation, dependance, and hope from themfelves con-
demned and flain by the law: therefore it is called, a killing
letter. The life-giving Spirit, is the gofpel, or that infinite
love, and difpenfation of grace: where the commandment is
fulfilled in Chrift: where all requifites, as repentance, faith,
love, &c. are produced in him, and the punifhment as perfectly
adequate to our offences fuftained by him. This, is Spirit, as
being the alone work of the Spirit, wrought in Chrift; and
perfectly free from the fpot of human righteoufnefs. This being the quickening Spirit, it is faid to give life, becaufe it
gives the perfect falvation of Jefus, freely unto fuch who are
dead by the law. And thus it is, that the letter killeth, but
the Spirit giveth life. With what propriety then, can any
man call the written word of God wherein thofe things are
contained, a dead letter? or wherefore muft the perfon who
believes, what he reads in the fcriptures, be accounted of as
a miftaken man?

mine which, but rather have waited for the day of decifion.

But as the knowledge, and enjoyments, which are yet future, with refpect to fuch as me; were prefent to this author, (if you will believe him) and are fo now to his difciples—he immediately determines the matter, by affirming, that neither a part, nor the whole, of mankind fhall be faved. He declares that the perfons of mankind are neither faved nor damned, that they are neither hated, nor loved of God: but, that it is the good and evil which is in them, that God loves, and hates, which he faves and damns.

" God, faith he, hates no man's perfon,
" but the evil in the perfon: neither doth he
" love any man's perfon, any further than as
" they fhew forth fomething of himfelf; as
" they were created by him: and in this fenfe
" he loves all creatures." I look upon this firft chapter of his *Advancement of all things in Chrift*, to be a compleat compendium of his whole fyftem. All the fruit of his labours, the produce of his wifdom and knowledge, ftands here delineated, and may without prejudice, or critical narrownefs, be fummed up, and perfectly comprehended in the following propofition.

God at firft, put forth mankind, and all creatures, as an outward image, or form of himfelf, and fowed the feed of eternity, or planted *Chrift* the good principle in them: but evil taking place in time, they had two oppofite qualities, or principles in them: and thefe two principles, conftitute the different characters, which are applied to the perfons of men,

E   as

as believer, and unbeliever, &c. they alfo
conftitute the characters of *Chrift*, and *Belial*,
&c. After the will of God is accomplifhed
upon them, man dies : and in the article of
death, *Chrift*, or the good principle, or quality, returns to God, and is abforpt in him,
whilft the evil principle is deftroyed in his
wrath. As for the perfon of man, that being
only erected as a ftage, for thofe principles to
combat each other upon for a feafon, (for
whofe diverfion, I cannot pretend to fay) it is
thrown down in death, and being there annihilated, it perifhes eternally as a beaft.

This is a perfect anatomy of his body of divinity, not fomething meerly deducible from
his writings ; but what he in fundry parts of
his works, has pofitively affirmed for truth :
This he hath cloathed with confequent propofitions, fuch as denying the perfonality of
Chrift, the refurrection of the body, and the
falvation of man's perfon.

He faith, that the perfon of man, is no
more than a beaft, and hath no pre-eminence
above a beaft. From hence it follows, that
there is nothing loft, nor faved, but the good
and evil qualities in man. As thefe qualities
are no part of man, but are, by him, diftinguifhed from the perfons of men, it follows,
that the perfons of men are not at all interefted in
the fate of either : Nay, he fays, that the perfons of men, hath only the portion of a beaft,
to die and be no more.

As we muft neceffarily lofe all intelligence,
and confcioufnefs of exiftence, in the lofs of
our perfons, it remains to be afked, for what
purpofe

purpofe were we created? wherefore was man
diftinguifhed from the brute, by being poffeffed
of the powers of thinking, reafoning, reflecting,
hoping, fearing, &c.? Wherefore the defire of
immortality, and the perfect averfion to anni-
hilation, which we feel within us? To what
purpofe did *Coppin* himfelf write; and what was
his hope under the perfecutions, which he re-
ports to have met with in the world?

Is this, the falvation that he hath promifed to
all mankind? Truly they are not much obliged
to him: I believe, that the generality of thofe
who think, will not thank him for the tidings
he brings to their ears, nor once bid him God
fpeed. But fuch inconfiftent, and horrible
whims, are ever the confequence of men's for-
faking their own mercies, to follow lying
vanities.

And yet there are thofe, whofe attachment,
to the opinion of univerfal falvation, is fuch,
that rather than part with it, they will be con-
tent, that fome very minute part of them only,
fhall be faved: Or, with *Coppin*, that only
fome principle of good, in them, fhall be faved, whilft their perfons fhall perifh everlaftingly: Yea, they would rather that the whole
race of *Adam*, fhould be annihilated, than that
all fhould not be faved.

The caufe of which, is eafily difcovered:
They are a people, whofe confcience reproaches
their conduct, and will not fuffer them to have
any hope from themfelves. They are alfo def-
titute of that faith in *Chrift*, which as the evidence
of things unfeen, and the fubftance of things
hoped for; gives affurance of perfonal intereft in

E 2   the

the falvation of Jefus.—Thus, that they might not be left as perfons without hope ; neceffity compels them to have recourfe to the opinion of univerfal falvation.

I do not mean that this is the cafe with all, who are of this opinion : there may be fome, who though well.perfuaded of their own perfonal intereft, in the falvation of *Chrift* ; are yet touched with fympathy, and compaffion for their fellow-creatures : and feeing nothing in themfelves better than others, perceive no reafon why others fhould not be benefited by *Chrift* as well as themfelves. They may alfo reafon from the riches of divine love, from the all-fufficiency of redemption by the blood of *Jefus, &c.* But after all, this opinion is not effential to their happinefs ; they do not make a point of it ; nor would they in the leaft refpect, facrifice the glory and honour of our Saviour to it: They may defire, hope, and think, but they are not pofitive. It would be uncharitable, and cruel, to cenfure fuch as thofe, whofe *hearts* feem to be right with the Lord.

It is therefore rather to the ferious confideration of the former, than to the latter, that I would recommend the following objections to their darling opinion : as they confift with the fcriptures, and with reafon.

I will begin with a queftion once propofed to our Saviour upon this head : *Lord, are there few, that be faved?* Luke xiii. 24. It is certain that the perfon who afked the queftion, had drawn fuch conclufions from the doctrines, which he had heard *Chrift* preach. Remark the Lord's anfwer : *Strive to enter in at the ftrait gate: for many, I*

fay

say unto you, will seek to enter in, and shall not be able. Doth not our Saviour seem to approve of this person's ideas, and to confirm them rather, by his answer? or what are we to understand by the strait gate; through which but few comparatively enter?

Again, *But if our gospel be hid, it is hid to them that are lost,* 2 Cor. iv. 3. That all men do not believe the gospel, or that it is hidden from some; is so very notorious, that it requires no proof from me. It remains for us then, only to enquire into the meaning of the term *lost,* as it is applied in the text. First, it cannot intend our being lost in *Adam,* for that would be to make the apostle say, if our gospel be hid, it is hid to them who are lost in *Adam:* But all mankind are lost in *Adam;* and yet the gospel is not hidden from all mankind: as appears from the distinction made in the text. Doth not the term *lost,* in the text, relate to the present and future misery of such, who believe not the glorious gospel of the son of God? if not, what does it then relate to?

Again, our Saviour saith, *If ye believe not that I am, ye shall die in your sins.* And again, *Whither I go, ye cannot come,* John viii. 24, 21. As it is needless for me to attempt proving, that all mankind do not believe in *Jesus:* we have only to consider the meaning of those words: *Ye shall die in your sins. Whither I go, ye cannot come.* What does a person's being in his sins intend? does it not imply a guilty conscience, unwashed, impure, and miserable: a conscience not believing, not apprehending the great salvation: and therefore as unhappy through ignorance, and unbelief, as if the Saviour had

E 3

not died, and rifen again? Is not living and dying in this ftate; what is meant by dying in
their fins? and if they die in their fins, wherefore fhould it be fuppofed, that their ftate is
changed in the article of death? Is not this
afcribing the glory, and honour of our Saviour,
to death; which is an enemy? If a man was
to die a thoufand times, he will not be the hap-
pier for that. True happinefs confifts in beholding the glory of God, in the face of *Jefus Chrift*. It is not by death, that we believe
the gofpel, but by faith, which is the gift of God,
and which cometh by hearing. It is not death,
that purifies the heart, and purgeth the confcience from dead works: but the blood of our
Lord *Jefus Chrift*. It is not by death, that we
are changed, but it is by beholding the glory of
the fon of God.

Thus death, cannot in any fenfe, be faid to
be our Saviour. If death infallibly cured all ills,
and rendered every foul happy that paffed
through it; it would be advifeable for all the
miferable to fly to it with fpeed: as they would
find in death a fure refuge from all diftrefs*.

How

---

* To be, or not be: that is the queftion;
  Whether 'tis nobler in the mind to fuffer
  The flings and arrows of outrageous fortune,
  Or to take arms againft a fea of troubles,
  And by oppofing end them. To die, to fleep——
  To fleep perchance to dream: ay, there's the rub;
  For in that fleep of death what dreams may come,
  When we have fhuffled off this mortal coil,
  Muft give us paufe: there's the refpect
  That makes calamity of fo long life.

For

How shall we understand those words : *Whither I go, ye cannot come?* do it not suppose, that there are some, who at death, cannot enter into that glorious bliss, where Jesus is gone? If this, is not the meaning of the words, I would gladly know what the true meaning is.

Again, Our Saviour saith, *Marvel not at this, for the hour is coming, in which all that are in the graves shall hear his voice, and shall come forth, they that have done good, unto the resurrection of life; and they that have done evil, unto the resurrection of damnation,* John v. 28, 29. Doth not this intend the future resurrection of the body? As to what *Coppin* says upon these words, I pay no attention at all to it, because it is unscriptural, and irrational. If it is objected that the grave in scripture, signifies hell. I answer, it doth not intend it here, for two reasons. First it is in the plural number; *i. e. graves,* which it never is, where it intends hell. Secondly, we read here of good and bad, coming out of their *graves;* which cannot be applied

ed

For who would bear the whips and scorns of time,
Th' oppressors wrong, the proud man's contumely,
The pangs of despis'd love, the law's delay,
The insolence of office, and the spurns
That patient merit of the unworthy takes,
When he himself might his *quietus* make
With a bare bodkin? Who would fardels bear,
To groan and sweat under a weary life,
But that the dread of something after death,
(That undiscovered country, from whose bourn
No traveller returns) puzzles the will,
And makes us rather bear those ills we have,
Than fly to others that we know not of?

E 4   SHAKESPEAR.

ed to hell: becaufe it is not fuppofed, that fuch who have done good, are in hell: and therefore cannot come forth thence.

It will be objected poffibly, that the term *graves*, is figurative; and implies that darknefs, and ignorance, wherein we are dead and buried by nature: and from which, we are brought forth in the perfon, and falvation of *Jefus*. I anfwer, fometimes the term *graves*, as ufed in the fcriptures, may be underftood thus: as in the 37th of *Ezekiel*, &c. But this doth not appear to be its meaning in the text before us, for two reafons. Firft, here are two diftinct characters, raifed out of their graves: they that have done good, and they who have done evil: which cannot be applied to that, which is raifed in the perfon, and falvation of *Jefus*; becaufe thofe only were raifed by him, who were dead in trefpaffes and fins. Secondly, It is fpoken of as a future matter, *the hour is coming*, &c. whereas our falvation in him, was not future, but prefent as well: And refpecting the purpofe, execution, and manifeftation thereof; it may be faid, to be that which *was*, which *is*, and which is to come. Thus fpeaks our Lord, ver. 25. *Verily, verily I fay unto you, the hour is coming, and* now is, *when the dead fhall hear the voice of the fon of God: and they that hear fhall live.* There is a very manifeft difference, between faying the hour is coming, and *now is:* and that of faying only, the hour is coming. The former intends the prefent, as well as the future; but the latter intends the future only; the former, by propofing, that what now *is*, is yet coming, bears witnefs of a divine progreffion; in quickning mankind

to

to the knowledge of the truth : But the latter, speaking in the future tense *only*, relates wholly to the refurrection of the body.

If it fhould be objected, upon *Coppin's* principles, that thofe terms, they that have done good, and they that have done evil, do not relate to the perfons of mankind : but to the principles of good and evil, which are naturally in every man ; and which are raifed, the one to falvation, and the other to damnation.

I anfwer, it muft firft be proved that the evil principle was dead, and buried in man, before it can be faid to be raifed : And here lies a great difficulty, becaufe there are fo many witneffes to prove, that the evil principle has been always alive in them, and therefore needed no refurrection ; *when I would do good, evil is prefent with me.* Good and evil, being qualities only, or principles, as *Coppin* calls them ; they bear no perfonal characters in the fcripture : But the characters mentioned in the text, are perfonal ; and therefore cannot intend the qualities of good, and evil. Would it be fenfe, to fay of the principle of good, they fhall arife to the refurrection of life ? or of the principle of evil, they fhall arife to the refurrection of damnation ? Good and evil, as qualities, or principles in man, have none other mode of exiftence, than by the actions, words, thoughts, inclinations, defires, &c. of the perfon in whom they are : feperate them from the perfons, and they lofe their mode of exiftence, and become names without meaning. Good, and evil, as applied to man, have the perfons, faculties, and fruits of mankind, for their fubftantives :

and

and it is eafily feen, that the ufe, meaning, and exiftence of the adjective, depends upon the fubftantive: So do the terms, good, and evil, when applied to man, depend upon their perfons and conduct.

How extravagantly filly, muft it then be, to talk of raifing, faving, or damning, the meer principles, or properties of good, and evil: diftinct, and feparate from the perfons of mankind! To talk in that manner, is indeed fo to fight, as one that beateth the air.

Laying afide all partiality, and prejudice, doth it not appear that the text under confideration, hath this meaning? There is a day approaching, when the Almighty *Jefus*, by the fame all-powerful word, which in the beginning, fpake the things which are, out of nothing, into materiality: fhall call the dead to life again. That they fhall all arife, refpecting good, or evil; or that ftate of confcience wherein they died, in the fame ftate they were in, when they laid down the body* : And that

their

---

* I would not be mifunderftood, as if I meant that the foul dies, or fleeps with the body until the refurrection. No: God forbid! as a chriftian I am affured from the fcriptures, and as a man, I am perfuaded from reafon; of the contrary. But, where I fay, that the dead will arife, refpecting the confcience, in the fame ftate wherein they died: I mean, that it is the blood of our Lord *Jefus Chrift* (and not death) that is the fountain opened for fin, and for uncleannefs. To fuppofe that mankind are faved in the article of death, whether they have believed on the Lord *Jefus* or not: is to make death a purgatory; through which, whoever paffeth is made meet for the kingdom of God: or otherwife it fuppofeth, that all iniquity, and oppofition to God,

is

their expectations will be according. Some, as
confcious of falvation; arife in full expectation
of a glorious immortality: whilft others,
confcious only of their fins, arife in woeful expectation of damnation! I fay, doth not this
appear to be the fimple, genuine meaning of
the text? As to the characters, they that have
done good, and they that have done evil; that
fpirit who gathers with *Chrift*, can eafily account for thefe: They who have done good, are
thofe, who believing on the fon of God, and
properly apprehending him; appropriate his
obedience,

---

is of the body; and confequently dies with it: or elfe, it is
to imagine, that God, not only reverfes his decree; but alfo
for their fakes, inverts the order of things; by making them
happy without believing on his Son : by feeding them with
bread which they have not eaten, or by warming them with
a garment which they have not put on : but the minors are
falfe, as contrary to fcripture and reafon; and therefore the
major is not true. Mankind are naturally miferable, and if
they do not all feel it, it is owing to fuch things in life, as
divert their thoughts and attentions from it: as ambition,
honour, power, riches, pleafure, diverfions, &c. But in
death, all thefe are cut off from man; and he is left to miferable reflections, and feelings. This muft be the cafe with all
who die in their fins; *i. e.* without the faith, and knowledge,
of their fins being done away, by the blood of *Jefus:* Their
ignorance and unbelief is hell; and as fuch it will be felt,
when there remains nothing to divert the attention from it.
And as we know of no difpenfation, for their delivery, between death, and the reftitution of all things; therefore was
it, that I faid: They would rife, refpecting good, or evil,
or their ftate of confcience; in the ftate they were in, when
they laid down their body. If it fhould be afked, whether
it is not poffible, for fuch who were once believers in *Jefus*;
to lie down in forrow? and whether they will remain in that
ftate of mifery wherein they died? I anfwer, that, which
from

obedience, and sufferings: and thus by union with him, are conscious of *his* good doings; in which consciousness, they live, and die, and rise again. They who have done evil are the contrary character; they believe not, they appropriate not ; they are only conscious of their own works, &c. which being all evil, they are characterized accordingly.

I might quote many other passages of scripture, as objections to the opinion of universal salvation ; but as they are all of like nature with those already mentioned, I shall mention no more of them here ; but shall now, offer
                                                                such

---

from the fears, terrors, and complaints of a dying person, may appear very dark to the survivors; may yet be cleared up to the afflicted, before they have left the body : and when they are incapable of giving standers-by, any account thereof. As in the mariner's compass, when the needle, which is touched by the loadstone; is set upon the pivot, it naturally points towards the north; nor will it stand to any other point, without a force put upon it: So the real christian, is a person whose heart the Lord hath touched, and *Christ* is the pole to which it points. If it is left to the bias which is given it by the divine contact, it will not bear to any other point: Therefore, whenever we find the heart thus touched, varying from its pole, we conclude; that it is held by *some* malignant power, contrary to its spiritual bias : Should this continue until death, which may be the case with some ; the power which restrained the heart, is then broken ; and it gladly returns to *Christ* the center of all its joys. Thus, though the enemy may for a time, make the christian heart vary from its pole; by working upon their bodily infirmities : such as nervous disorders, melancholy, lunacy, phrensy, idiotism, deliriums in fevers, &c. Yet death frees the soul from all these; and administers an entrance for it into the fulness of that bliss, which, at any time it had tasted, in the knowledge of the son of God. This, is the difference in death, between the christian, and the infidel.

fuch objections, as reafon and common fenfe fuggefts, to this opinion. Doth not the opinion of univerfal falvation, fuppofe; that the irreligious, and unbelieving part of mankind; hath greatly the advantage of others? The Pfalmift faith of the former, *They are not in trouble as other men : neither are they plagued like other men.* If all, who die, go immediately to glory; then the ftate of that perfon, who paffeth through life, without thought, without conviction, without fear, without temptation, without reproach, without perfecution, &c. which is the ftate of an unthinking infidel, of the man of pleafure, the worfhipper of the God of this world: I fay, the ftate of fuch a perfon, muft be vaftly preferable, to that of the religious man, *i, e.* of the true believer. The apoftle faith of the latter, We *were troubled on every fide : without fightings; within fears.* They are troubled with the plague of a corrupt heart; (of which others are not convinced) they are troubled with the temptations of *Satan*; (whereas in others, the ftrong man armed keeping his palace, all his goods are in peace) they are troubled from without; hated, defpifed, and perfecuted in life. But, if unbelievers, and defpifers, are equally advantaged with them in death; then inftead of gaining by the faith of the fon of God, we fuffer lofs : which God forbid!

This argument, will be anfwered, with faying: That where troubles abound, as in the true chriftian, confolations much more abound: and that the happinefs, which a believer feels, through the faith of the fon of God, much

more

more than compenſates for all the afflictions, which he has ſuſtained more than other men. That there are unſpeakable conſolations in the knowledge of the ſon of God, I readily confeſs : and, that there is ſomething in the religion of *Jeſus*, ſo delightful, and ſatisfactory to the mind, that ſuch who know it, cannot chuſe but think, and ſay, that if there was nothing far-ther than the grave, it is preferable to all that this world can afford. But this is not always the caſe ; let it be remembered here, that the religion of *Jeſus* propoſes a future ſtate ; and ſuch a ſtate is believed, by thoſe who make their confeſſion as above. Beſides, every chriſtian hath not equal conſolations : There are ſome, who are children of affliction all their days ; ſubject to bondage, and to the fear of death ; and are yet dependant on *Jeſus*, under a particular diſ-penſation. Again, the generality of thoſe who talk much of their happineſs, are but proud boaſters ; they have taken up chriſtianity, as a ſyſtem ; they know nothing of themſelves, and, not having *Chriſt* revealed in them, by the Spi-rit, there is no oppoſition from the enemy : they are not plagued as other men ; but being of chearful, joyous diſpoſitions, they think themſelves perfectly aſſured, of matters which they know nothing at all of. Such as theſe cannot ſay with the apoſtle, *If we had only hope in this life, we ſhould be of all men moſt miſerable.* Neither the prophets, nor apoſtles, ever pro-poſed, that the enjoyments which we have, of divine matters, over balances the diſtreſſes, which every real chriſtian meets with in life ; but quite the reverſe. Hence it is, that we are

directed

directed to that, far more exceeding and eternal weight of glory, which remains for us; in comparifon of which, our prefent afflictions indeed are but light; but they would be heavy enough, if we had no *future* expectations.

Again, if according, to the opinion of univerfal falvation; all mankind went immediately through death, to glory: the fcriptures are of no ufe, they have been continued unto us, to no purpofe; and the preaching of the gofpel is vain. If all are equally faved, unto what purpofe do we read, and ftudy the fcriptures; befeeching our Saviour, to give us a true underftanding of them? poffibly it will be anfwered, they might as well be let alone; every man might fpare himfelf the pains of reading and ftudying them; fince when they come to die, they would be equally as well off as *Paul*, or *Peter*, or any other of the apoftles who wrote them.—Is not this a true ftate of the cafe, if the abovementioned opinion be true. But leaft any one, fhould, through the ftupor of this opinion, neglect the great falvation; and find themfelves moft miferably deceived when they come to die. Let us treat the matter ferioufly, as being of fome importance.

We muft acknowledge, that, through a feries of divine providence, the holy fcriptures have been continued to us even to this day: And that, though they have paffed through the hands, not only of fuch, who believe not the true gofpel, but even through the hands of fuch who are enemies to chriftianity in general; yet they have not been loft. This is the Lord's doing, and its marvelous in our eyes. Our

Saviour

Saviour bids us fearch them, for they teftify of him. But to what purpofe were they continued unto us, and wherefore did the Lord bid us ftudy them ; if they were not defigned to be our guide, and directory, and to make us wife unto falvation ? But, if all, are faved at death, the fcriptures are of no ufe ; and our Saviour's advice to read them, to fearch them, is altogether unimportant.

Again, if the opinion of every man's entering into glory when they die, be true ; would it not be truly politic, to imbibe the popular fentiment, though it fhould be with the denial of Chrift ? By that means we fhould avoid, the cenfure, calumny, reproach, hatred, and condemnation of the world ; which otherwife falls upon us, for our fentiments, and manners. From what fuch who call themfelves chriftians, have imbibed from heathen philofophers ; I may expect this objection. A chriftian, without having any view to future matters, loves truth, and makes choice of it for its own fake ; when at the fame time he knows he fhould be altogether as happy after death, if he defpifed it, and poured the utmoft contempt upon it. To this argument, there are two very material objections. The one from the nature of man, and the other from the nature of God. Firft, I think the compliment a great deal to high, which is paid to human nature : in making it capable of loving virtue for its own fake. (Excepting that man who laid down his life for his enemies) I may challenge proof, that any one individual of *Adam*'s race, in any one action of life, were perfectly detached from felf. The
apoftle

apoftle tells us, that *Mofes*, when he forfook
Pharaoh's court, to fuffer affliction with the
people of God ; had *refpect unto the recompence of
the reward.* There is not one action of our
lives, however difinterefted, and generous it
may feem; but what we promife fome advantage, fome confolation or pleafure to ourfelves
by it. Hence I affirm, that the profeffion,
of loving truth, or virtue, meerly for its own
fake, is theory, only ; altogether without
practice.

Again, fhould it be granted, that mankind
may act from their love to truth ; for its own
fake : as this would be obedience in the fuper-
lative degree; fhall we not fuppofe that the
divine Being, holy, righteous, and equitable as
he is, would diftinguifh fuch a fpirit; and in
fome fenfe manifeft his approbation of it? But
this is not done in life, according to the teftimony of experience, and of the fcriptures :
Since the fame events happen to the one, as to
the other ; and if all are equally happy when
they die, it is not done then : which would be
to fuppofe that good, and evil, are alike to
God. A propofition, blafphemous in itfelf,
and highly difhonourable to the divine Being.

Again, if this opinion be true, wherefore did
our Saviour fend forth his difciples, into all the
world, to preach the gofpel to every creature?
and wherefore did the apoftles, martyrs, and
confeffors of *Jefus*, fuffer the moft cruel torments, and even *death* for his name fake? If
all, were to be equally happy in death, the
apoftles certainly preached in vain : for mankind had all been faved, had they been filent.

F   It

It had been more genuine mercy, not to have disturbed the world, with the animosities, and bloody persecutions, which took place upon preaching the gospel; nor to have distressed individuals, by interrupting their peace, and repose, with convictions, and manifold troubles. Wherefore did the apostles, under innumerable hardships, labour incessantly, to bring souls to the knowledge of the truth, since if they had left them alone, they had been equally happy?

If the latter be the case, the apostles, confessors, and martyrs of *Jesus*; were guilty of the most egregious folly, in subjecting themselves to such hardships as they did; in giving their bodies to be stoned, to be beheaded, burned, crucified, &c. for a testimony, the belief of which, gave them no advantage above any one of the human race: A testimony, which, if they had recanted, and denied, it could not have prevented their happiness.

Again, it makes void, and totally destroys all divine retaliations*. With what reason, or

from

---

* It may not be unnecessary to distinguish here, between grace; and providence: according to the former, God having concluded all under sin; the free gift is upon all men, unto justification of life. But even here, a man cannot fill his belly with the east wind: he cannot have any personal happiness, until believing in the son of God, he knows his personal interest in the great salvation. When this is apprehended, whether the person was a bloody persecutor, a rapacious publican, an avowed enemy of God, of Christ; of mankind, &c. before; or not: it makes no difference, because, it is seen here, that all manner of sin and blasphemy is forgiven unto men. He who owes but fifty pence, is not

more

from what revelation, can we fuppofe, that the mocking infidel, the bloody perfecutor, the barbarous, the cruel,the avowed enemy of God, of *Chrift*, and of mankind, fhall when they die, though they die in the fame ftate wherein they lived; be equally happy with *Paul, Peter, John,* &c. ? I would afk the chriftian, can any man be happy by *Jefus Chrift*, without believing on him ? And let me alfo afk the Infidel, can any man be happy on the principles of human goodnefs, without being poffeffed of that goodnefs ? Thou forgaveft them

---

more frankly forgiven, than him who owed five hundred pence. *Paul* fpeaking of himfelf, fays—who was before a blafphemer, and a perfecutor, and injurious; but I obtained mercy becaufe I did it ignorantly in unbelief, 1 *Tim.* i. 13. The mercy which he obtained, exempted him from guilt, and condemnation; but not from the retaliations of providence: for he, who with a mercilefs and unrelenting eye had beheld the torments of his fellow-creatures; and had even been an abettor, and affiftant, in ftoning the martyr *Stephen:* was ftoned himfelf at *Lyftra*, and drawn out of the city for dead—He who had purfued the difciples of *Jefus* with the fury of the deftroyer, even unto cities remote from *Jerufalem*; was purfued, himfelf; by the *Jewifh* nation, in the elders of the people, in *Ananias* the high-prieft, and in *Tertullus* the orator, even unto *Cefarea:* where they accufed him before *Felix*, as a blafphemer, &c. a man worthy of death. He, who was ufed to make havock of the church, haling men, and women to prifon: was in procefs of time, upon the very fame principles, caft into prifon himfelf. When *David* finned heinoufly againft the laws of fociety; in defiling the wife of a faithful fervant; and then, to cover his fhame, murdering the innocent worthy hufband; by the hand of the children of *Ammon:* even then the prophet pronounced his iniquity forgiven: but gave him to underftand that the fword fhould not depart from his houfe: which probably occafioned this faying; Thou waft a God that forgaveft them, though thou tookeft vengeance of their inventions, *Pf.* xcix. 8. Nor

was

them (faith the Pfalmift) but thou tookeft vengeance on their inventions. But we do not always fee thofe characters retaliated in this life; on the contrary, they flourifh as a green bay tree: but it is unreafonable to fuppofe, that when they die, they fhall be equally happy with *Noah*, *Daniel*, and *Job*.

Again, hath not this opinion a bad effect upon the minds of mankind? doth it not make them loofe, frothy, and carelefs? doth it not teach them to laugh at ferioufnefs, to defpife, and make a jeft of divine matters? do they not
from

---

was it long before *Tamar* the daughter of *David*, was deflowered by her brother *Amnon*—and when this grief began a little to fubfide; behold *Amnon* is murdered by *Abfalom*, and the murderer becomes an exile. When time had in a meafure erafed the memory of this evil, and partly affwaged the grief of the king; lo *Abfalom* was permitted to return. Soon after he raifed a rebellion againft his father; chafed him from his royal palace, and from his beloved capital; and then entring into his father's houfe, he fpread a tent upon the top thereof, and lay with his wives before all *Ifrael*: Nor, did *David*'s troubles ceafe, when *Abfalom* was dead. From thefe, and many more inftances which I might mention from the fcriptures; we may obferve that there is a diftinction to be made between grace, and providence. The former pardons all, as fin againft God; but the latter, one time or other, retaliates refpecting our behaviour towards our brethren, or fellow-creatures. And if faith in Chrift, the knowledge of the forgivenefs of fins, doth not exempt perfons from fuch a retaliation; as appears from *David*, *Paul*, &c. what muft be the end of fuch who believe not the gofpel, but are rather enemies to it all their days? We do not fee that they always meet with retaliations in this life. The pfalmift fays, that they are not plagued as other men: but to fuppofe, that thofe who live, and die in fuch a ftate, fhall enter into glory, without meeting any retaliation at all, is to impeach divine juftice and equity, and to make God a refpecter of perfons; which God forbid, that any man fhould think.

from hence, neglect the fcriptures; and pre-
ferring their own opinions, defpife the gofpel
of our Lord *Jefus Chrift*? In brief, do they not
by means of this opinion, lofe what they had attained unto; and fink into infidelity, or what is
as bad, dwindle into an unthinking, ftupid,
carelefs ftate: and all from the opinion of univerfal falvation? Doth it not encourage the ufe
of unlawful means, as fuicide, &c. to efcape
prefent trouble; by entring into that blifs, unto
which it pretends to entitle all mankind?

Again, it deftroys the nature, properties, and
ufe of faith: by deriving all hope, and certainty
of future blifs, from falfe reafoning.—Having
firft laid down this propofition, All mankind
fhall be faved: what follows, but this conclu-
fion; if every man is faved, I fhall be faved?
But the major is not proved; therefore the
hope, and comfort, which is drawn from the
minor, is precarious, and unfatisfactory. But
faith is of a divine original, it is not fomething
acquired; it is the gift of God: it confifts of
light, perfuafion, and power: its properties are
to make manifeft, to perfuade, and to evidence
the truth of unfeen things; to repel oppofition; to lean, truft, hope, and depend on ma-
nifefted truth; and to affure the mind of future
blifs, from the veracity of the divine record.
As light, it manifefts *Jefus Chrift* in the
heart; according to the fcripture report of him
as our Redeemer and Saviour: it perfuades us
of the truth, of what we difcover, it repels
our fears, and falfe reafonings, and gives us
joy and peace in believing. This is not of our-

felves,

felves, but of the free gift and operation of God our Saviour.

But to conclude, that we fhall be faved, upon the fuppofition that all fhall be faved; hath no faith at all in it: but it is a low reafoning, a reafoning from very great uncertainties; from an opinion that hath no foundation in revelation. Therefore I faid, it made void faith; which indeed it does, and alfo the preaching of the gofpel; and the hearing of the word, by which faith comes; as I have already fhewn.

Thefe are a few of the many objections, occurring to my mind; againft the opinion of univerfal falvation. And thefe, I fubmit to the ferious confideration of thofe, who are attached to that opinion.

I think I have now done with *Coppin's* works; except a few remarks, which I fhall make upon the preface, to his book intitled, *The advancement of all things in Chrift*, &c.

Mr. *Cayley*, the author of this preface, in order to recommend the book, more effectually, tells us, that it was written above an hundred years ago. Pray what dependance hath truth upon antiquity, or wherein confifts the neceffary connection? Is it neceffary to our happinefs that we fhould be antiquarians in divinity; or was that book written in an ÆRA of time, when men were infallible? Mr. *Cayley* pretends, that the defign of his writing the preface, (was for the fake of weak brethren) to remove their prejudices, &c. And here I cannot but obferve; that he muft have a high opinion of himfelf, even beyond all rules of proportion; to fuppofe, that his very name would frighten

the

the adverfary, and remove the prejudices of
the weak brethren : befides which, we have nothing but his bare word, for the glorious
truth contained in this book. Mr. *Cayley* tells
the reader, that, if he is a father in *Chrift*, the
unction of God, in him, will witnefs to the
truth, without any other argument. What a prodigious thing, felf-importance is! We are fathers in *Chrift*, if we think as Mr. *Cayley* does ;
if we rejoice with him, to fee fo glorious a teftimony ; if the unction within us witnefs to the
truth of it, without any other argument. I
would gladly know, whether the unction in Mr.
Cayley witneffed to the truth of it, without his
reading it; for, needing not his confeffion, I
am well perfuaded, that he did not attend to
any argument, neither from reafon, nor fcripture,
when he fet about recommending it.

Either Mr. *Cayley* perufed this book before he
prefaced it, or he did not : If he did read it,
he either underftood it, or he did not underftand it : If he did not underftand it, with what
face of honefty could he recommend it ? If he
did underftand it,, and recommend it, he muft
be fuppofed to be of the fame principles with
thofe which I have expofed ; and I hope con-
futed. But if he recommended it with fo much
warmth, without reading and confidering it,
which I almoft fufpect, from his pretending,
that fathers in *Chrift* (of which he is no fmall
one in his own conceit) know the truth of
books, without attending to argument. I fay,
if he did this, I cannot but confider him as an
enthufiaft, if not fomething worfe.

But

But what if we cannot palate, cannot digeſt this precious morſel? Why then according to Mr. *Cayley*, we are babes, meer little-ones, who as yet feed on milk, and know not how to di-geſt ſtrong meat ; not having as yet, our ſpiri-tual ſenſes exerciſed, to diſcern between the myſtery of good and evil. The apoſtle ſaith, *Not a novice, leaſt being lifted up with pride, he fall into the condemnation of the devil.* Was I called upon to give my opinion of the novice character, I would do it thus: A novice, is a perſon of but ſmall experience in the knowledge of God, or of himſelf. Hence he arrogates characters, and authorities, diſallowed of by God and man : he expects that you ſhould im-plicitly receive his ſayings, or what he recom-mends for truth : he would perſuade mankind, that he is poſſeſſed of an unerring unction : by which, without attending to argument, or ma-king any uſe thereof, he knows, writes, and ſpeaks the truth infallibly. Hence it follows, that whoſo receives not his ſayings, are abſo-lutely babes, have no knowledge of ſpiritual things, *&c.* I need not ſay that this is a being lifted up with pride ; and with ſuch pride, as is very nearly related to the devil's pride ; a ſpiri-tual pride, productive of oppoſition, to the perſon of the ſon of God. Mr. *Cayley* charges the babes, the little-ones, to beware of judging, or cenſuring what they underſtand not; which by the way, is to tell them that do not ap-prove of it, that the fault lies altogether in *their* underſtanding, for that the book is faultleſs. As to his cautions, advice, *&c.* I think them ſufficiently impertinent, as applied to the read-

ing

ing of human compofitions; for I know of no
faith, or credit, which we owe them; any farther than they confift with the word of truth;
and with the argument of reafon: and where
the latter is not the cafe, we are at liberty to
reject them as error, or nonfenfe, whoever the
writer be. He charges us, to be fo reafonable,
as to embrace what we can comprehend; and
what is out of our reach, to leave it to God,
and judge it not: perhaps what is dark to-day,
may be light to-morrow. What a perfon is
convinced of, comprehends, and believes to be
true, that he naturally embraces: advice upon
this head, is therefore needlefs. As to our not
judging what is out of our reach, but leaving
it to God; I would obferve, that what is out
of the reach, of our experience, may not be
out of the reach of our underftanding: therefore we are at liberty to judge of the truth of a
propofition, from its rationality, confiftency,
&c. without having recourfe to our experience;
i. e. to fuch operations and effects, produced
in our minds, as are perfectly correfpondent
with fuch a propofition. Every reafonable man,
has a right to judge of the truth of what he
reads, in the former fenfe, though he may be a
ftranger to the latter. Therefore, though what
Mr. *Coppin* and Mr. *Cayley* fays, may be out of
our reach; refpecting the experience of it; it
cannot be out of the reach of any reafonable
man; refpecting its rationality, confiftency, and
confonancy with fcripture; according to thefe
he hath a right to judge of it.

As to his faying, what is dark to-day, may
be light to-morrow; I fee not how it relates to

truth

truth and error, for they are always the fame.
Jefus Chrift is not yea and nay; he is the fame
yefterday, to-day, and forever: but that
which oppofeth him, is darknefs to-day, and
to-morrow alfo. Beware, faith he, of pinning
thy faith on any man's fleeve ; (a poor unmeaning faying!) Learn to fee the Sun of
righteoufnefs (faith he) with thine own eyes,
and not through another man's fpectacles,
which may deceive thee. A faying of the fame
nature with the former, but intended as a cau-
tion to us, againft thinking ; or feeing things
in a different light from Mr. *Cayley*.

I would defire thee, O reader! (faith he) to
take notice, that the fpirit, which breathes in
the following treatife, is nothing but *glory to God
on high, and on earth, peace and good will towards
men :* which is the true mark of a gofpel-fpirit.

I muft confefs, that I had once a better opinion of Mr. *Cayley*'s judgment. I could not
have thought, that he would with fo much
confident warmth, have recommended a book fo
very repugnant to the fcriptures : and even to
common fenfe. But there is one thing to be faid
indeed on his behalf : that he does not attend to
argument ; or to what the book fays, fo much,
as he does to the breathings of the fpirit in it.
But whether the book, or the fpirit that
breathes in it, has deferved the character given
it by Mr. *Cayley*, I have already fhewn in the
courfe of my remarks upon it. If denying the
body of *Chrift*, the perfon of *Chrift*, the refurrection,
and afcenfion of Chrift, the falvation of Chrift;
the refurrection of *our* bodies, the falvation of *our*
perfons. I fay, if thefe glorify God in the higheft,
&c,

&c. then Mr. *Coppin* has done it; and Mr. *Cayley* is not a falfe witnefs; otherwife, the contrary is manifeft. But whether thefe doctrines, and this fpirit, breathes glory to God on high, peace upon earth, and good-will towards men; or not, judge all ye people. Here (faith he) is no encouragement to fin, but great encouragement to finners, *to behold the Lamb of God, who taketh away the fin of the world.* In fhort, in this book, (faith he) there is contained a *feaft of fat things,* furnifhed with what is fuitable both to men and babes. Is it poffible, that Mr. *Cayley* fhould be fo greatly charmed; and that he fhould have fuch a prodigious relifh for things which he did not underftand : Nay, let us rather in a judgment of charity fuppofe, that he did perfectly underftand it; and that when he read it, he not only found it to be favoury, but to be the moft delicious food to his foul. Such a fuppofition, and none but fuch, will excufe that fervent zeal, with which he recommends it. Let us alfo imagine, that it is from hence, he declares, that there is no encouragement to fin in it.

What encouragement it may be to fin, in telling a man that his body fhall not rife again, that God neither hates, nor loves his perfon; that his perfon is neither the object of falvation, nor damnation; that every man hath in him, the principles of good and evil; and that the good principle fhall be faved, and the evil one loft : I fay, what encouragement thefe may be to fin, I fhall leave to others to determine. But I am very well affured, that there is no encouragement given to finners : to look to the

Lamb

Lamb of God who taketh away the fin of the
world, as he infinuates; becaufe firft, in denying the perfonality of the Lamb of God, and
that falvation from fin, which is by his facrifice
upon the crofs; he *deftroys* him, and fets up in
his ftead, a creature of his own fancy; a meer
calf, gilded with the fuppofition of a good
principle in man. Mr. *Cayley* will call this the
Lamb of God, if he pleafes, but it is not the
perfon whom *John the Baptift*, called the Lamb
of God, that is certain : nor does looking to the
Lamb of God, in Mr. *Cayley*'s fenfe, intend any
thing more, than a man's looking to himfelf.
But here, again, I am almoft tempted to think,
that he does not perfectly underftand the fyftem
which he has adopted; for according to *Coppin*,
man is no more a finner than the beaft that perifhes. The perfon of man, is neither good nor
evil; but only a theatre, a temporary conveni-
ence, whereon thofe jarring elements, thofe oppofite principles, and powers, make war upon
each other for a feafon; the perfon of man, being quite neutral, hath nothing to do in the
affair.

Oh reader (faith he) do not fall out at table,
and turn this feaft into a battle, by rafh judg-
ings, and cenfurings, of what thou cannot yet
underftand.

I fincerely afk my friend *Cayley*'s pardon, if
I appear as one, who falls out at table. It is
becaufe he hath invited me to a feaft where
there is nothing to eat : but what I (fuppofing
myfelf poffibly, as good a judge as himfelf)
know to be unpalatable, and unwholefome:
and this, to a perfon of appetite, is no fmall
disap-

difappointment. I am not quarelling, but giving
my reafons only, why I cannot partake of his
feaft; which I take to be a point of good manners, where I am with fo much earneftnefs
preffed to eat.

Poffibly, the title page of the book, which
Mr. *Cayley* prefaced, was not a fmall induce-
ment to his doing it; where we are told that
the book contains *fome fparkles of that glory, and
fome beams of that light, which fhines and dwells in
Richard Coppin.* What an enthufiaftic, and antichriftian puff, this is! O *Paul!* you were but
a babe, when compared with thefe apoftles. I
do not remember to have read any fuch language in your writings, as this: being fome
fparkles, of that glory, and fome beams of that
light, that fhines and dwells in me *Paul.* Nay,
but you taught, and yet teaches, that all the
fparkles of glory, and beams of light, fhines
and dwells in *Jefus Chrift:* who is the fun of
righteoufnefs, the bright, and the morning-
ftar.

Thine, O great apoftle, was the fpirit of
truth: Thou beareft not witnefs of thyfelf;
though if any man had whereof he might glory
in the flefh, thou hadft more: But thou glori-
fiedft *Jefus,* by receiving of the things which
were his, and fhewing them unto us: It was thy
bufinefs to efpoufe mankind to one hufband, as
a chafte virgin to *Chrift.*

But not fo Mr. *Coppin,* who talks of fparkles
of glory, and beams of light fhining and
dwelling in himfelf; he bears witnefs of himfelf, and his witnefs is not true.

If

If Mr. *Cayley*, or any of *Coppin's* admirers, think that I have mifreprefented them, let them not only impute it to my ignorance, but let them convince me of it. It lies particularly upon Mr. *Cayley* to do it; by giving us a proper comment upon *Coppin*; and in fo doing, he will act up to his own memento, at the clofe of his preface; nor has he any juft reafon, to think of me otherwife, than as his fincere friend, and well-wifher.

FINIS.

www.ingramcontent.com/pod-product-compliance
Lightning Source LLC
Chambersburg PA
CBHW032248080426
42735CB00008B/1049